Profit in Guinea Pigs
Breeding, Management and Practical Knowledge of Cavies

by Dr. J.A. Roberts, DVM

with an introduction by Jackson Chambers

This work contains material that was originally published in 1922.

This publication is within the Public Domain.

*This edition is reprinted for educational purposes
and in accordance with all applicable Federal Laws.*

Introduction Copyright 2018 by Jackson Chambers

Self Reliance Books

Get more historic titles on animal and stock breeding, gardening and old fashioned skills by visiting us at:

http://selfreliancebooks.blogspot.com/

Introduction

I am pleased to present yet another title in the "Cavies" series.

The work is in the Public Domain and is re-printed here in accordance with Federal Laws.

Though this work is a century old it contains much information on bees that is still pertinent today.

As with all reprinted books of this age that are intended to perfectly reproduce the original edition, considerable pains and effort had to be undertaken to correct fading and sometimes outright damage to existing proofs of this title. At times, this task is quite monumental, requiring an almost total "rebuilding" of some pages from digital proofs of multiple copies. Despite this, imperfections still sometimes exist in the final proof and may detract from the visual appearance of the text.

I hope you enjoy reading this book as much as I enjoyed making it available to readers again.

Jackson Chambers

DR. J. A. ROBERTS
Judge, Writer, Lecturer and Breeder of Cavies.
Pacific Coast Secretary
of
The Western Cavy Breeders' Association.

CONTENTS

	Page
Introduction	9
Cavies (Poem)	10
Origin of Cavy	13
Development of Cavy	13
Commercial Use of Cavies	17
Cavies for Food	20
Cavies for Fur	25
Housing of Cavies	29
Feeding of Cavies	35
Breeding of Laboratory Cavies	42
Exhibition of Cavies	45
Grooming and Preparing for Exhibition	46
Cavy Breeders' Association (Article)	48
Ailments of Cavies	50
Summary	55
Meat and Fur Production (Article)	71
Breeding of Show Cavies	74
Judging Show Cavies (Article)	81
Guinea Pig Industry (Article)	87
Climate and Cavies (Article)	90
Cavy Industry of the South	93

CAVIARY AND STOCK BARN
Formerly Owned by the Author.

Introduction

The subject of Cavies is one that has attracted worldwide attention, and there are many ideas advanced along different lines. We shall try and give you in plain words our opinions as to securing the best results and success in raising Cavies, and also pertaining to the Cavy Industry.

Cavies offer unlimited possibilities to the public, and as the cavy industry is practically in its infancy at the present time, there is a wonderful chance to get into the field when it is young and make considerable money, depending, of course, on the number and the quality of stock you start with and also regarding the increase, which is large, for cavies breed faster than any other animal.

The raising of cavies is one of the most fascinating propositions known, and in order that this book may be accurate and complete as possible, I have not hesitated to approach various specialists; and in this connection I am particularly indebted to the following gentlemen, all of whom are up-to-date breeders of the modern cavy: Mr. E. D. Wheeler, Secretary of the Western Cavy Breeders' Association; Mr. E. D. Corrin, President of the Western Cavy Breeders' Association; Judge Lewis S. J. Griffin, Mr. E. G. Haberstroh, Cavy Experts; Otto M. Locke, Jr., Southern Cavy Expert and Chief Judge; Chas. S. Gibson, Organizer of the National Breeders' and Fanciers' Association, Inc.

Cavies

Cavies are small, but of great importance to us all,
Some people contract diseases and hear the death call.
Many have died in the past years who we knew,
And you never can tell—the next may be you.

Many died because science at that time did not find
It could produce serums from cavies of every kind.
Many a soldier and person who lives today
Owe their lives to the cavy in just this way.

Cavies have brought gladness to many a home,
In cases of sickness—not only alone,
But wealth they have brought to many breeders,
And they will do the same for you, my dear readers.

If you do not neglect them and will care for them well,
Then you will have numerous cavies to sell,
As they are easy to raise, the work not hard to do,
And a thousand breeding sows can be cared for by you.

Always select good stock when you start in to buy,
Then the offspring will be strong and will seldom die.
It pays any one when starting in to buy the best,
Because this class of stock will always stand the test.

No business in the world was built in one day,
But time, patience and persistence will pave the way.
Cavy raising I am sure you will enjoy,
And no matter how many, they never annoy.

It is not like raising poultry that you attend to a lot,
And get up at night to see if the incubator is too hot,
For the days may be cold and the wind may blow,
But the cavies will bear young for a fact, you know.

PROFIT IN GUINEA PIGS

Hens fail to lay if the weather is not right,
But the cavies will have their young, even at night.
The hen will earn one dollar in a year, perhaps two,
But figure for yourself what the cavy will do.

Get into a business that is young like this,
Then there will be no chance for you to miss.
You will share in the profits of the industry now,
And be selling your stock at $5.00 per sow.

Join the Western Cavy Breeders' Association,
And they will give you all the necessary information
As to promoting the cavy industry in the United States,
Also the big shows held various places on certain dates.

—By DR. J. A. ROBERTS.

WHITE PERUVIAN MALE

Origin of Cavy

GUINEA PIGS are native to South America. In their wild state they are slightly smaller than our domestic guinea pig and of an ugly, grayish-brown color. In the sixteenth century they were taken by the Spaniards into Europe, where they underwent considerable change in the process of domestication. However, they are still hunted in South America by the natives and are considered one of their best game foods. They live around trees and cliffs. Guinea pigs found in North America were mostly brought from Europe. Previous to the arrival of Europeans on the West Coast of South America there were only a few domestic animals which could be used as food. The guinea pig was one of them, so you can see that the cavies were of great importnce as a food supply. We are told that the Indians had great numbers of cavies in and about their houses.

It can be safely said that the general knowledge of the origin is very limited.

The wide interest shown in cavies during the war goes to show the value of these little animals. Guinea pigs played a very important part in our last war, and also previous wars. Many a wounded soldier owes his life to one of these little animals.

DEVELOPMENT OF CAVY

It has not been until late years that people have put forth great efforts to bring out the possibilities of the variation of colors and setting aside a certain standard to work on. In color, cavies were described as all white and all yellow.

PROFIT IN GUINEA PIGS

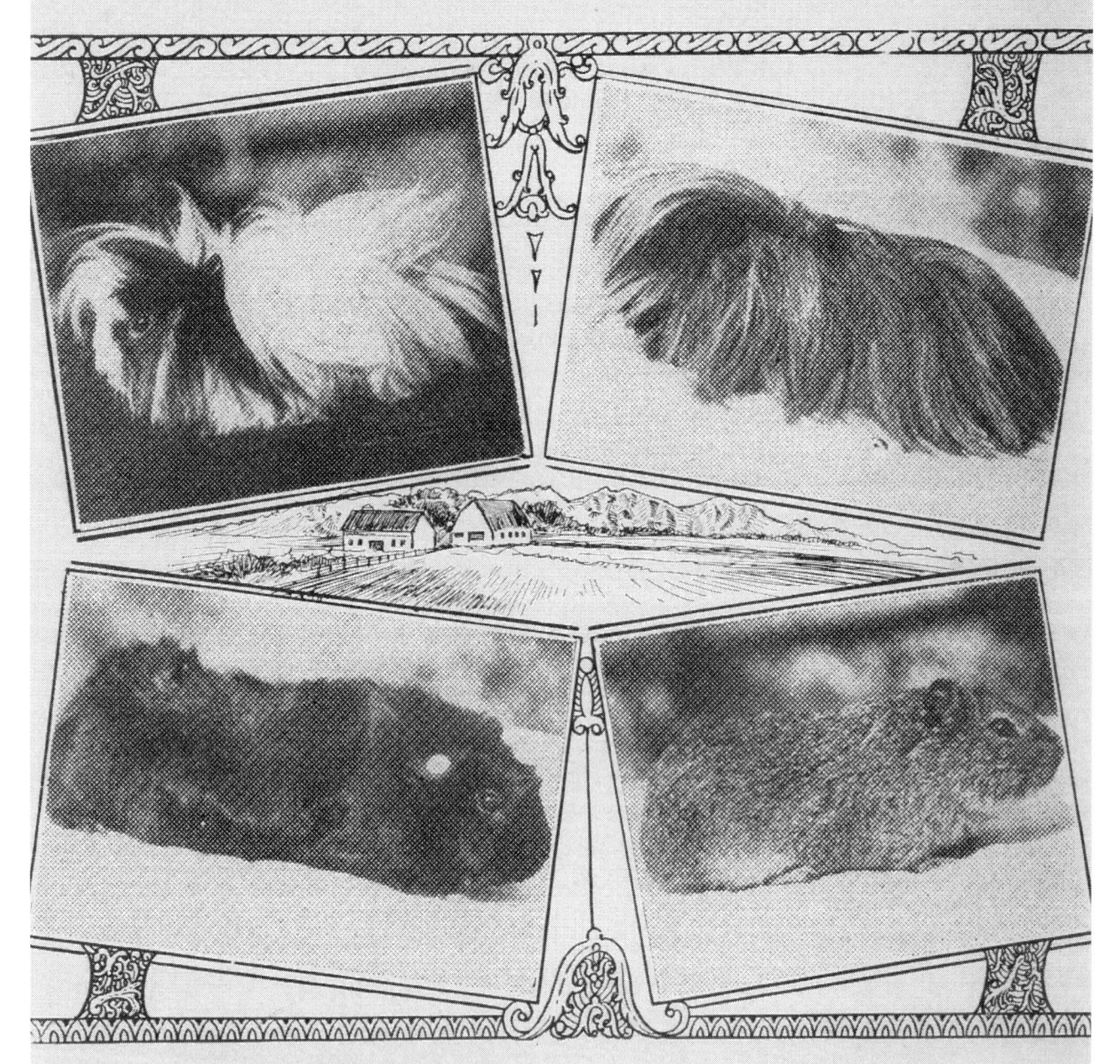

Upper Left—BLACK AND WHITE PERUVIAN FEMALE.
Upper Right—BLACK PERUVIAN MALE.
Lower Left—BLACK ABYSSINIAN. (Note Rosettes.)
Lower Right—SILVER AGOUTI CHAMPION MALE.
The Above Are Show Stock.
The Short-Haired Breeds Are More Desirable for Laboratories.

PROFIT IN GUINEA PIGS

A confusion of colors, lacking definition, adorned the coats of the old-time guinea pig. Today they are bred to a principle, reproduce faithfully, and, as year succeeds year, one sees the introduction and establishment of new, distinct, beautiful sub-varieties. Color is brilliant, deep, pure and charming; markings are brought to an established standard; coats in the smooth-haired varieties are of a short and silky nature, while in some of the self-colored varieties, such as blacks and reds, the color is carried right down to the toes, and even to the toe-nails. A standard of perfection in breeding exhibition cavies today has become a science upon well-defined lines. Points in shape are developed and bred with unerring accuracy; colors are purified and intensified with success, astonishing even to specialists themselves. The eye of the old-time guinea pig would contrast in size to that of the modern cavy almost as a pea to a bean. Again, there has been wonderful development in the process of breeding for size, head properties, and general contour. All round there are the same evidences of modernity and advancement in the animal itself.

Standards of excellence are drawn up, shows held, and others encouraged by the gift of special prizes, and in a hundred and one ways the development of the cavy fancy has progressed.

There are varied specimens of cavies; some are smooth haired, which are called the English; medium long haired, which are called Abyssinian, and the long haired, which are called the Peruvian, and come in many colors. Below you will find a classification of the Western Cavy Breeders' Association:

1. Abyssinian—White.
2. Abyssinian—Black.
3. Abyssinian—Red.
4. Abyssinian—Cream.

PROFIT IN GUINEA PIGS

5. Abyssinian—Golden Agouti.
6. Abyssinian—Broken colors.
7. English—White.
8. English—Black.
9. English—Red.
10. English—Cream.
11. English—Chocolate.
12. English—Tortoiseshell.
13. English—Tortoise and White.
14. English—Silver Agouti.
15. English—Golden Agouti.
16. English—Himalayans.
17. English—Dutch.
18. English—Blue.
19. English—Brindle.
20. English—Broken colors.
21. Peruvians—Black.
22. Peruvians—White.
23. Peruvians—Red.
24. Peruvians—Creams.
25. Peruvians—Broken colors.
26. Angora (Peruvian Silkies).
27. Miscellaneous.

HAPPY AND CONTENTED

Don't Scratch, Bite or Burrow.

Commercial Use of Cavies

THE uses of cavies are many, and a classification of same would be: Laboratory uses, which is the largest; Food, which is becoming of more importance each year, and Fur. Under the heading of Laboratory purposes would come the making up of the various serums and antitoxins to combat the various diseases, such as pneumonia, typhoid fever, scarlet fever, diphtheria, malarial diseases, camp fevers, and many serums that are not entirely perfected at the present time.

DUTCH BELTED ENGLISH CAVIES

Every city, village or town in the entire United States all use serums made from cavies to counteract the effect of the above mentioned diseases. During the war every soldier who went across, and many in this country, received from 4 to 27 injections of serum. The laboratory use, therefore, is considered the largest and

PROFIT IN GUINEA PIGS

is steadily increasing each year. There are over fourteen hundred laboratories, colleges and institutions in the United States that at certain times of the year use a great number of cavies.

People are coming to realize that serums are the real means of overcoming many diseases, and the demand for same is becoming more pronounced each year. The United States Government issues a Bulletin, put out by the Agricultural Department, called "Guinea Pigs or Cavies, Farmer Bulletin No. 525." Any one can secure a copy of this Bulletin by writing them.

Until recently Guinea Pigs were raised only as pets, and to some extent for food. They do not bite or scratch as some cats and dogs do, and because of this gentle and harmless nature they have been, and are still, great favorite as pets for children. In the past few years, however, it has been discovered that Guinea Pigs are excellently adapted for experimental purposes in such work as testing and standardizing serums and antitoxins, in medical research work and in certain tests for ascertaining the presence of disease germs.

ABYSSINIAN, BROKEN COLORED

PROFIT IN GUINEA PIGS

They are rapidly taking the place of white mice and rats for this purpose and the demand is rapidly increasing. They are used daily in thousands of hospitals, laboratories and colleges. This big demand, which is so much greater than the supply, explains why this new industry has come into existence and why there is so much to be realized from the raising of these little animals. As medical research advances and the manufacture of serums and antitoxins increases, the demand for Guinea Pigs will be enormous, and those who make a business of supplying this demand are sure to get good returns for their investment. For example, we quote below a portion of an article published in a popular local newspaper recently:

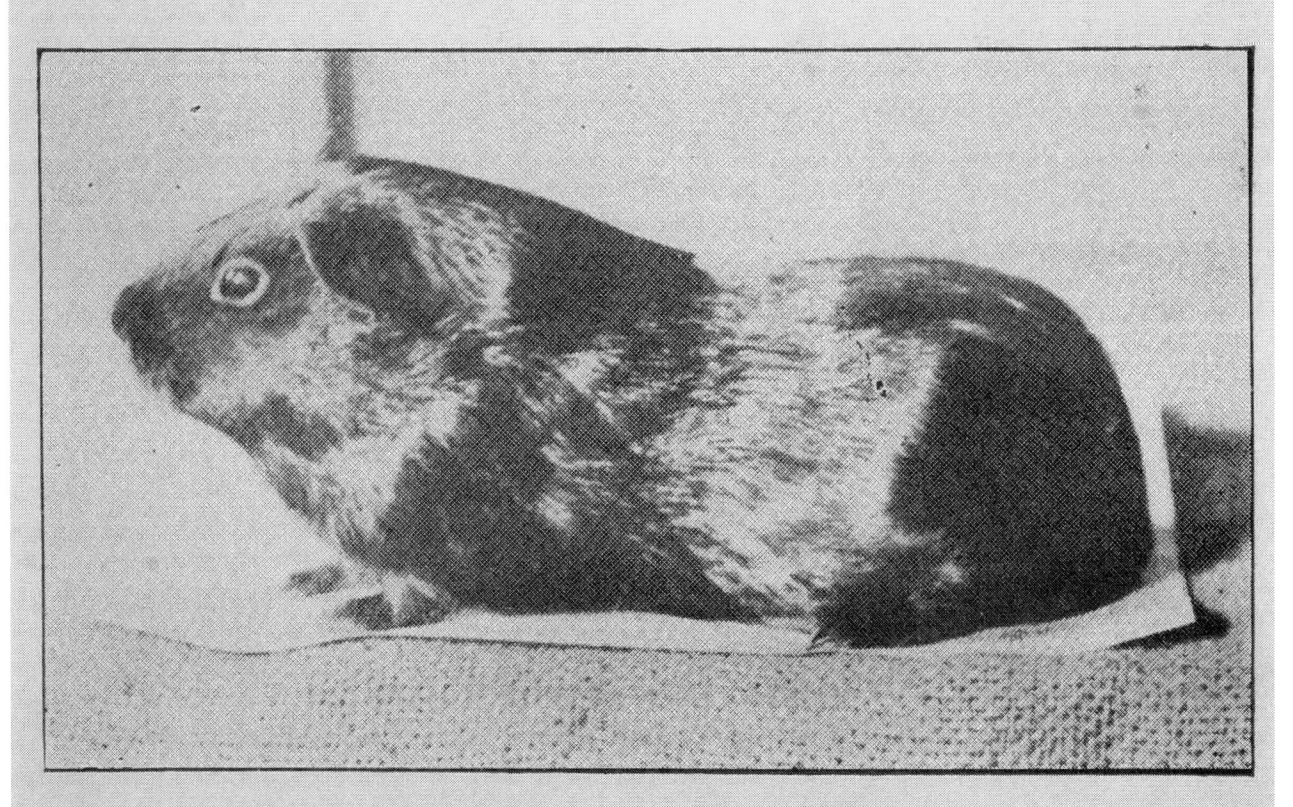

BLACK ENGLISH SOW
Imported

PROFIT IN GUINEA PIGS

GUINEA PIGS DIE THAT FILIPINO BABIES MAY LIVE

Scientific Feeding Experiments to Determine Good Native Food from Bad.

MANILA, P. I.—Fifty guinea pigs are in a special room in the Bureau of Science building in Manila feasting to their hearts' content to teach a staff of food specialists what Filipino diets are good and what ones are worthless.

They constitute a part of the force working under the direction of Miss Hartlee Embrey, food chemist for the Rockefeller Foundation, who is here experimenting with food products in the Philippines in an effort to work out a balanced ration which will not cost the average Filipino a price out of his reach.

Part of the guinea pigs eat one diet, while others feast on another. Some of them are fat as guinea pigs can get, while others are skinny and still others are dying with scurvy. The latter classes are martyrs to the cause. They are dying that Filipino babies may live.

The effect of the foods under study on them will teach the food specialists, and through them the general public, that these foods are not to be eaten.

CAVY AS FOOD

There can be no doubt that once the general public becomes convinced of the suitability of the cavy for table purposes, a great impetus would be given to cavy breeding, as we all know, according to history, that cavies were the chief food of the Spaniards and that Europe has used the cavy as food for the last century. We have little doubt that before long no poultry show will be complete without classes for cavies. This is now largely an accomplished fact, and we have good

PROFIT IN GUINEA PIGS

reasons to hope that at a time not far distant cavy, in some of its savory and delicious preparations, will be considered requisite in good menus. Many of the largest and finest hotels in the United States are now serving cavies, prepared in various ways, and a great many eating places are substituting cavy legs for frog legs, for there is not one in a thousand that can tell the difference. In this case they use the hind legs of the young cavy which is about one month old. There are a few concerns that put them up in cans, which are labeled "Pork Cavy Soup." However, there are numerous ways of canning them so as to give them a variety of flavors and adding vegetables to suit the taste.

PREPARING THE CAVY.—The cavy can either be skinned, or simply scrape the hair off and prepare with the skin on. It is rather difficult to scrape the hair off, as they must be scalded in water of 180° F., and the hair scraped off with a knife; but this is difficult to do if the water is too hot. When the hair is removed, open the cavy and clean the same as a chicken or any other small animal. If one does not care to clean these animals themselves, they can take them to their butcher, who will kill and prepare them for cooking.

We will give you a few recipes below which we are sure you will enjoy:

"EXCELLENT CURRY.—Peel one Spanish onion, one small carrot; pare and core one large, rather sour, apple; mince these very fine and put them, with one ounce of butter, into an enameled stewpan; fry to a golden brown, dredge in a tablespoonful of flour and let them take a rather high color; add ¾ pint of good stock, a pinch of celery seed, a small faggot of sweet herbs and a piece of garlic no larger than a pea. Stew for three hours. A full-grown cavy having been prepared for cooking, cut it up into joints and rub them with a tablespoonful of curry powder. The powder should not

PROFIT IN GUINEA PIGS

be very hot. Stir in the gravy as a puree through a coarse sieve, return it to the stewpan, add the cavy and curry powder, and salt to taste; bring it to a boil and immediately draw it back from the fire, letting it stew slowly, till the skin of the cavy is gelatinous and the flesh parts freely from the bone. If the gravy is too thick, moisten with a little stock; if too thin, take out the cavy and boil down till it is of the right consistency. See that it is properly salted and serve in an entree dish, with rice boiled dry in another dish."

"The cavy makes an excellent white stock for veloute, white soup, etc.; for this purpose the cavies should be full-grown. It is needless to urge upon good cooks the

MOTHER CAVY WITH YOUNG ONE DAY OLD

value of a viand that will answer this purpose. A very nice, clear soup can be made by boiling down a couple of large cavies, with vegetables, to a consomme, and serving in it the prime joints of one or two delicate young cavies which have been thoroughly stewed.

PROFIT IN GUINEA PIGS

Cavy makes excellent pie, either to be eaten hot or cold, but should be stewed before being put into the pie, unless the pie be of the old English kind, with a short crust, and is baked a long time in a slow oven. In boiled pudding it is also very good. The pudding should be well boiled."

"**CAVY AUX FINES HERBES.**—Take a full-grown and fat hog cavy, killed, scalded and cleaned as previously described. Blanch it in one pint of boiling water, cut it into joints; make the water thick with a white roux of butter and flour. Put it over the fire in a moderate-sized stewpan; stir till thick and quite smooth; add one tablespoonful of parsley and one of green onions or chives, chopped small, and pepper and salt to taste; stew the cavy in this for two hours, or until it is perfectly tender. If a pint of stock be used instead of the water, this dish will be much improved; thicken with the yolk of an egg, and serve."

TORTOISE AND WHITE MALE CAVY

"**BROWN SOUP.**—Place a large, fat cavy in two quarts of water, with vegetables; a middling-sized onion, cut into rings and fried brown; pepper and salt to taste, a small blade of mace and two teaspoonfuls of mushroom ketchup. Stew for four or five hours over a brisk fire, keeping the quantity of soup up to two quarts by adding boiling water occasionally. Strain the stock through a wire sieve, and thicken it with a brown roux. Have ready the best joints of two small cavies. Stew these very gently in the thickened stock until quite tender. The flavor may have diminished in the long cooking and some more seasoning may be required. Serve very hot, with fried toast, cut in dice."

FRIED CAVY.—Wash and cut up a young cavy, season with salt and pepper, dredge with flour, or dip each piece in beaten egg and then in cracker crumbs. Put in a frying pan one ounce each of butter and sweet lard made boiling hot. Lay in the cavy and fry brown on both sides. Take up, drain it and set aside in a covered dish.

Stir into the gravy left, if not too much, one tablespoon flour, make it smooth, add a cup of rich milk or cream, season with salt and pepper, boil up, and either pour over cavy or serve separately, as desired. Some like chopped parsley added to the gravy.

CAVY EN CASSEROLE.—1 tender cavy, ½ cup Crisco, salt and pepper, 1 cup hot water, 1 cup hot sweet milk or cream, 2 cups chopped mushrooms, 1 tablespoon chopped parsley.

Clean and skin cavy. Either cut up or split and lay in casserole. Spread over with Crisco, dust with salt and pepper, add hot water, cover closely and cook in hot oven about 45 minutes, or until done. When nearly tender, put in rich milk or cream, mushrooms and parsley. Cover again and cook about 20 minutes longer. Serve hot in the casserole. Oysters are sometimes substituted for mushrooms and will be found to impart a pleasing flavor.

PROFIT IN GUINEA PIGS

FRICASEE OF CAVY.—Prepare and cut up as for fried cavy. Put in sauce pan with just enough boiling water to cover; add a teaspoon of salt, a little pepper, and, if desired, a teaspoon of onion juice. Boil slowly until tender; add a little water from time to time as it boils away. Thicken with a tablespoon of flour mixed with a little milk or cream, and add a tablespoon of finely chopped parsley. Serve plain, or with border of hot boiled rice or dumplings.

STEWED CAVY.—Melt 4 tablespoons Crisco or lard in saucepan; joint cavy and fry quickly in hot grease, then fry 1 sliced onion until browned, stir in 2 tablespoons flour and brown flour; now add gradually 2 cups water and stir until smooth. When boiling add salt, pepper and paprika to taste, and 2 tablespoons chopped parsley; simmer slowly 1½ hours. Dish and strain over gravy.

CAVIES FOR FUR

Cavy fur is being used at the present time, but not extensively, by a number of fur factories that substitute it for various kinds of fur. We believe that some time, without a doubt, there will be a season for the cavy fur, depending, of course, on the coöperation of the various cavy breeders throughout the United States, as there is no animal known that you can get the variation of colors from as you can from the guinea pig, or cavy.

The public at this age is looking for effective colors, and coats and furs made from the cavy skins are unusually attractive. We have a lot of breeders report to us that they have made automobile robes, gloves, scarfs, coats and numerous articles from cavy fur. It is beautiful and soft and glossy. The cavy breeders throughout the United States are turning more to the fur market than in previous years, and many of them report fur companies writing them for cavy furs in large quantities.

PROFIT IN GUINEA PIGS

MRS. J. A. ROBERTS
KNOWN AS REEKA ROBERTS ON THE SCREEN.

PROFIT IN GUINEA PIGS

Personally, I believe the only drawback on the fur proposition at the present time is due to the fact that factories require the fur in such large quantities, and there is no one who can supply them, as most of the cavies are being used for laboratory purposes. The laboratories pay more for cavies than you can realize on the fur at the present time.

Cavies, when they are used in laboratories in standardizing serums, develop a high fever and temperature, which causes the hair to fall out, and for that reason

MRS. CHAS. S. GIBSON
Writer, Lecturer and
Judge of Fur

the fur cannot be used after the laboratory tests. Any business in the world depends on supply and demand. If the cavy breeders would coöperate and devote their time to advertising and talking the fur proposition, no

PROFIT IN GUINEA PIGS

doubt it would bring wonderful returns. The Western Cavy Breeders' Association, with headquarters at Colorado Springs, which has members throughout the entire United States, is doing a great deal in promoting the cavy for food and fur. The cavy industry is a very important thing in the United States at the present time and can be made more so by the co-operation of breeders. Therefore, I personally believe, you will be well paid for joining the above association and give a helping hand to the possibilities in this wonderful industry.

RED ENGLISH CHAMPION MALE

Housing of Cavies

A GREAT many ideas have been advanced along the lines of coops and hutches for cavies. However, I would advise all intending to raise cavies to provide themselves with good hutches that will be serviceable and handy in caring for their stock, as any kind of a hutch will not do. If you expect to become a successful breeder and exhibitor of cavies, you should have good housing facilities for raising.

We do not recommend outdoor hutches for cavies. It is better to have a small shed, garage, or some means of protection that is not draughty. However, if you have no other place to keep them than outside, we would suggest that you have your hutches built against a wall, so that they will have protection against draughts.

Hutches should be built at least ten inches off the ground, and have a roof over them. Outside hutches should have a roof projecting about two feet in front of the hutches, so that in damp or wet weather the feeding and cleaning out arrangements may be handled with the least amount of inconvenience and discomfort.

Cavies should also be protected from cats, dogs, rats, or any animal that will injure or destroy them. The floor of your indoor houses can have a dirt or concrete floor—it does not matter. Many poultrymen throughout the country convert their poultry houses into caviaries, building, of course, their hutches on the side that they will get the sunlight.

People should use their own judgment in regard to this situation. We believe that the best method as to housing is as follows: Build your hutches 2 feet wide

PROFIT IN GUINEA PIGS

by 4 feet long, using 1"x3" material. In these spaces of 2'x4' you should have two trays, each tray being two feet square. These trays should have side walls of three inches. You will note that the 1"x3" material is also used for these trays. The bottom of your trays should be built out of redwood or any light box lumber 5/8 inch thick. Between one hutch and the other you should use 1/2 inch square netting wire, which you can purchase at almost any hardware store, or screening will answer the same purpose; however, you should not use 1-inch poultry netting, for this is too large a mesh and the young pigs will crawl through.

You can build as many runs of hutches as you have space for and you can have them five hutches high, and this will be convenient in caring for them, for the top hutch will be five feet six inches from the floor. The space between one hutch and the one above can be 9 inches, 10 inches, or a foot, depending on the person who builds them.

It is not necessary to have any small boxes in the corner of your hutches for cavies to have young in, as is necessary for rabbits, as cavies would crowd into them, causing death of the young. Cavies, when they have young, select a corner of the hutch and the others will not interfere with them.

This space of hutch, as mentioned above (2'x4'), is capable of handling 4 females and 1 male, or 5 females and 1 male.

When it is necessary to clean your hutches, which should be done about once a week, you will note that by having the two trays in the space that the cavies will pass from one tray to the other, so that you can draw it out as you would a bureau drawer and dump the contents into a barrel, or whatever method you use in cleaning the hutches. This method of housing makes

PROFIT IN GUINEA PIGS

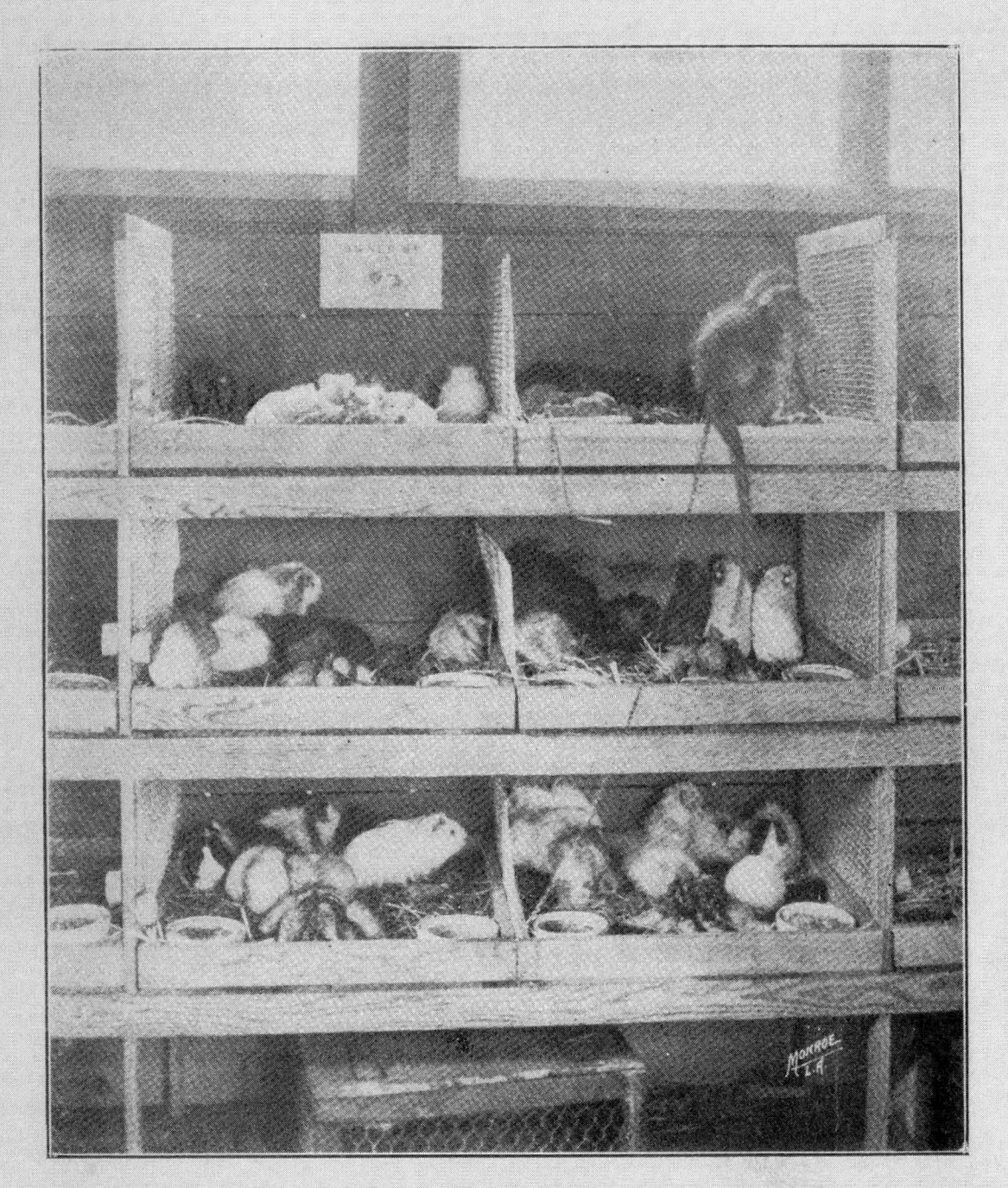

NOTE HOW HUTCHES ARE BUILT
This is one of the best housing facilities.

cavy raising no burden as to cleaning hutches. If you want to make two tiers of hutches together, you can use some wire as mentioned above between them. That is, for instance, a building 16'x30' long could have a

PROFIT IN GUINEA PIGS

double row of hutches in the center, and a building this size should be capable of housing one thousand breeders.

You can, if convenient, have a little sunlight for the young pigs, for any animal puts on rapid growth when they have access to the sun. However, by this we do not mean that cavies should have no protection from the direct or intense rays of the sun.

THIS HUTCH WILL HOLD 45 CAVIES—4 FEMALES AND 1 MALE IN EACH COMPARTMENT

Cavies naturally are afraid of falling. While some people do not use any doors or screen in front of their hutches, this is entirely up to the breeder. If you think your cavies will form a habit of jumping out of their hutches, then it is better to use coverings in the front. We will, however, quote the United States Government's bulletin on "Hutches and Pens":

"Two methods of managing guinea pigs have been advocated—courts and hutches. In court management the animals are kept in open or covered courts in which they have considerable room to exercise. The courts are divided into smaller runs, each of which has its own

PROFIT IN GUINEA PIGS

hutches or sleeping shelters. The size of the runs is governed by the number of animals to be kept in them. A run 6'x10' would accommodate 30 to 50 guinea pigs. In a warm climate court management has certain advantages. It entails less labor in feeding and cleaning than is required under hutch management. However, for most parts of the United States indoor hutch management is the only plan that can be recommended. In cold weather artificial heat should be supplied. In fact, guinea pigs do best when the temperature is not allowed to fall much below 65° F. It is true that they are often kept in outdoor hutches in winter, and that huddled together in warm nests and well fed they survive the low temperatures, but such management cannot be recommended. The animals do not thrive well under it, and there is a great danger of serious losses of the young through pneumonia. They should not be subjected to sudden changes of temperature or to dampness.

Guinea pigs require about the same kind of accommodations as rabbits. The same hutches would answer, but they may be smaller for guinea pigs. Those used by the Bureau of Animal Industry are about 20 inches wide at the front, 3½ feet deep, and 18 inches high. These accommodate a male, three or four breeding females, and their progeny until weaned. The compound hutch is suitable for producing cavies on a commercial scale. Each compartment is 30 inches deep by 36 inches long and has a floor space sufficient for five or six breeding females with their litters. The number of compartments in a compound hutch may vary more or less, according to the requirements of the breeder. The netting used on the large doors may be galvanized sand screen or poultry netting having a mesh not greater than three-fourths of an inch. In tiered hutches of this sort there should always be enough absorbent bedding to keep the floors dry. Cheaper hutches may be made of packing boxes laid on the side and fitted with a door in

PROFIT IN GUINEA PIGS

front, which would answer every requirement, but if many of the animals are to be raised in a limited space it is desirable to have hutches of uniform size.

"A shelf about 4 inches high is recommended for the darker part of each hutch. The space under the shelf is a convenient retreat for females that have young, while the shelf itself is nearly always chosen by the animals as a sleeping place.

"Another convenient and cheap plan for indoor runs, is an arrangement of two decks, of five runs each, the floor of the upper being about 4 feet above that of the lower. The space between the decks is open and the walls of the runs are made of boards a foot wide. Each run is 5 feet long and from 20 inches to 2 feet in width."

WORLD'S CHAMPION PERUVIAN
Owned and Exhibited by Roberts' Laboratories

Feeding of Cavies

THE feeding of guinea pigs is a very simple matter. Their main food is good, dry hay or grass, and their green food consists of any kind of food that is not harmful, such as alfalfa, barley, carrots, lettuce and cauliflower, etc. However, the green stuff should not be fed immediately after cutting. It should be allowed to wilt for about an hour or two before feeding. You should feed cavies the amount of green stuff that they can eat in about 20 minutes in the morning and 20 minutes in the evening. Green food should not be allowed to stay in their hutches at all times. This is where a lot of people make mistakes, by crowding green food into the hutches, which causes them to become damp, and is also a wasting of food.

We recommend feeding cavies green food twice a day. For example, morning and evening, and at noon give them a handful of hay. Bran should be kept before the cavies at all times. We recommend bran because it is a very cheap food and is a wonderful laxative and keeps cavies in a very healthy condition.

We do not recommend watering cavies when you are feeding them green food, as all green stuff contains about 95% water, and this is sufficient to take care of their needs. However, if you are feeding dry food entirely, then you should have water before your cavies at all times, except in cold weather, as explained in the following chapter. The city raiser can most always get lots of green stuff that the commission houses throw away. Stale bread is also very good food for cavies. We are, however, listing a classification of the various foods which will be of value to you as to the different varieties of food for the cavy:

PROFIT IN GUINEA PIGS

GREEN FOODS.—Lawn clippings, alfalfa (green), clover (green), lettuce, dandelions, carrots, celery tops or stalks, corn (green) or stalks, mangels, spinach, apples, cauliflower, weeds, kale, barley (green), etc. Do not feed green stuff too wet.

DRY FOODS.—Timothy hay, oat hay, clover, alfalfa, oats, bran, corn leaves, rolled barley, rolled oats, dry bread.

Might add, however, that green clover and alfalfa during the summer, when you can get it, is wonderful food for cavies.

WATERING CAVIES

The watering of the cavy is entirely up to the breeder. If you believe that your cavies will do better with water, try it out for a short time, especially if you are feeding

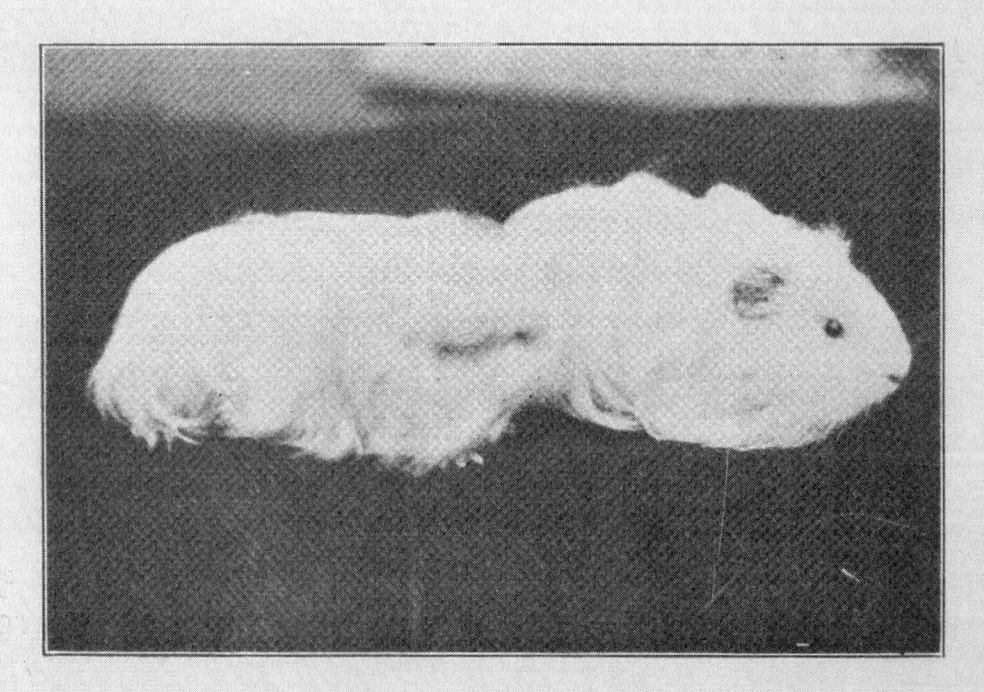

SILK EYE WHITE PERUVIANS
Winners Where Ever Shown

PROFIT IN GUINEA PIGS

them a considerable amount of dry food. Most authorities are about equally divided as to giving and not giving water.

In the summer time, during the hot weather, we believe that stock will do better with water. However, in the colder weather cavies are apt to get their noses wet and thus sometimes cause colds, which perhaps will terminate in pneumonia. However, as stated above, we would suggest that you use your own judgment.

In shipping the cavy, never place water in the shipping boxes.

BREEDING OF CAVIES
Show Stock.

This subject should not be confused with the breeding of laboratory stock, for the reason that show stock should not be bred as often as laboratory stock.

Gestation period of the cavy is 65 days, but it may vary a couple of days either way. You should mate your stock up in pens of four females and a male. Select the best specimens and watch which sows produce the best youngsters. In show stock you want less young, but good, hardy ones. Do likewise with the boars, find out your best boars that produce the best offspring. Sometimes a sow will breed winners to one boar and cavies of no merit whatever to another. Therefore, never part with a good sow until you have tested her with two or three boars.

Do not dispose of a boar that shows results in breeding color, size and shape, but select his male offspring and try to get the same results on the young stock. However, do not breed the young boars until they are six to eight months old, and have them in condition when you mate the stock. The condition is very impor-

PROFIT IN GUINEA PIGS

BLACK PERUVIAN MALE

PROFIT IN GUINEA PIGS

tant in show cavies at all times, and feeding has a lot to do in regard to making a success in breeding stock.

As to breeding age, avoid mating sows too early—six to eight months being ample time. Try and mate your sows to older boars. Some breeders let the male run with the females only about ten days, while some breeders leave the male with the females at all times. Do not breed two cavies that have the same faults.

BREEDING FOR COLORS.—Breed two cavies that have nearly the same marking if you wish stock to be of same color. Select your color markings and have a standard to go by and select your young accordingly, until you have your strains well developed in size, shape and markings.

BREEDING OF ABYSSINIAN CAVIES.—In this particular breed you should be very careful in selecting your male pigs, for the reason that they should be as near perfect as possible and their coats should be thickly covered with rosettes. You should breed the best quality females and also select your females with the most rosettes, as quality is bound to show in the breeding hutch, as well as the exhibition pens. You should try and select your foundation stock from breeders who have a reputation on this class of stock. It does not pay to buy them wherever you chose, as you should know their breeding qualifications. If you purchase faulty stock it will take years to overcome the defects.

A FEW GENERAL HINTS.—It is not well to handle your sows when they are heavy or around littering time, and in breeding show stock it is better to just breed two, or not more than three litters per year. Breeding show stock four or five times a year does not produce big, strong, healthy youngsters. In breeding this stock your aim is to produce size and conformation. Do not use your male cavies too much. A person wish-

PROFIT IN GUINEA PIGS

RIBBONS FROM THE PANAMA-PACIFIC EXPOSITION

PROFIT IN GUINEA PIGS

ing to enter into the breeding of show stock should not be in too great a hurry, as it takes a great deal of time and patience.

Many raisers, as I have stated before, leave their females all together; that is, four females and one male in a pen, while they have their young. This is not a good thing to do regarding this class of stock, but when you find a sow is getting heavy and near littering time, it is well that you separate her and place her in a pen by herself. However, I am not against sows littering together if you haven't sufficient room.

If a sow has more than three young, select the poorest stock and place them with another mother cavy. However, there are a great many ways in developing show stock; for instance, if you have a litter of cavies born and there is one or two of them that you are expecting to enter into a show and that you want to get considerable growth on them, it is well that you leave only two of the youngsters with the mother, so that they will receive more nourishment and grow faster. Always feed your sows extra food when they have young and give them considerable attention and plenty of nice, clean bedding. Young sows may be kept together and also adult sows when not in breeding pens, but you should part the boars when they are six weeks old, putting them in separate pens until they are about six months old, or older, and ready for breeding. Another very important thing is not to get your brood sows too fat, and do not overcrowd your stock at any time.

If you have some stock that you know is A1 and you are pretty sure no one can beat you, it would be well for you to save them for show purposes yourself, as it will give you considerable publicity and prestige that will enable you to receive high prices for your stock. If you have prospective purchasers around trying to buy your stock, do not be too anxious to sell. In selling cavies it requires considerable salesmanship; however, as stated above, do not be too anxious to sell; and whenever you do sell, do not consider that the cavy is your only object, but that you are also selling satisfaction.

BREEDING LABORATORY CAVIES. — This is entirely different from breeding show stock, as you do not have to take as much pains and be as careful in your selection and mating of stock. We do not mean by this, however, that you should neglect them, for to be a successful raiser and breeder it is necessary that you devote time and patience with any live stock.

Gestation period, as stated before, is sixty-five days, and cavies will breed immediately after having young; but it is better to let them wait a week or two weeks before breeding them, and young cavies are weaned at three weeks old. When you remove them from the pens they should be segregated according to sex, placing the males in one pen and the females in another. However, you should keep track of your different breedings so that you will not be confused in regard to the time you will be ready to mate up new pens of young breeding stock. However, you can breed laboratory stock any way you wish, except brother and sister. Breeding sire to offspring is line breeding, and some of the best stock in the country has been produced this way. The greatest strain of cattle in the country years ago was produced in this manner by Thomas Bates, the great shorthorn breeder of England.

Mating laboratory stock is similar to show stock — four females and one male. However, the laboratory stock you should leave together at all times, and with your hutches four feet high and two feet wide there is ample space for the four females to have young at the same time. Furthermore, it is a very good plan to have

PROFIT IN GUINEA PIGS

them all litter about the same time, as some females will have more young than others, and the cavy mothers will nurse each other's young; it does not matter. If you should happen to have a sow die a short time after littering, you can always save the young if you have another female that is nursing. Laboratory stock breed at two months of age; therefore, you can mate up your younger breeding stock at two months, but it is better to mate them with an older male, as this will produce more females to the litter, and as per records we have kept on a great number of breeders, they have produced 60% to 70% more females than males to litters, and, consequently, the females are worth more than males on account of breeding purposes. Laboratories throughout the country would just as soon have males for laboratory use as females, and in marketing your stock to the large laboratories it is necessary that you become a large raiser, so that you can supply them a certain number each week, or unless you are raising stock for a concern that do handle the laboratory trade. A great many of

RIBBONS WON BY CAVIES
Exhibited by E. D. Wheeler

the smaller laboratories throughout the country use a few cavies each week. However, one of these laboratories you could cater to nicely on a small scale. There are numerous concerns in the country that give out contracts to raisers that a great many raisers are connected with, and this assures them a market for their stock. Color markings do not make any difference in regard to laboratory stock, and the smooth English cavies are the ones that are used for this purpose.

You should be sure when purchasing your foundation cavies that they are not the offspring of undesirable stock, as a great many small laboratories do not take precautions in destroying cavies after they have used them for serum purposes and sell them outside, and this stock is of no use to any one or any laboratory, and they do not breed and thrive as they should, because their blood is affected with whatever serum antitoxin they were inoculated with.

Exhibition of Cavies

GREAT care should be taken in selecting your stock for the show. Many successful breeders make their plans from the very day they enter into breeding cavies for show purposes. That is to say, they start at the earliest possible moment in producing cavies for type, size and color.

In exhibiting smooth cavies, you should have as much gloss as possible on the animal's coat. If you can get your cavies to drink a little milk each day, this will help them greatly in producing glossy covering. The cavies must be sound and in perfect health, or it will disqualify their appearing. When you have a litter of young cavies that you wish to keep for show purposes, take out the smallest stock, or all except those that you figure on entering in the show. This will enable the stock to grow much faster and get more nourishment. Let this young stock run with the mother for a month or six weeks. When these youngsters reach two months of age they should be taken away and placed in a pen where they can have a lot of exercise. One of the features in showing cavies is steadiness; however, some stock is very wild and hard to handle. This makes it bad to judge them, and a judge cannot judge their merits properly. This condition arises because the breeder did not handle his stock sufficiently before exhibition. A well-trained animal in any show ring has the winning chance on the judging stand if its other points are equal.

SHIPPING CAVIES.—In shipping your cavies to the various shows, you should have your shipping coops of sufficient size and properly ventilated. Ventilation is a very important factor and should be arranged so as not to cause any draughts. A proper way for shipping show cavies is to bore one-half-inch holes close to the top of the box in each end. This will allow the air to pass in circulation without placing the cavy in draught. Stock should be shipped to the secretary of the association that is conducting the show and also have a return address, in case some one should make a mistake, and always label your shipping box "Live Cavies—Handle With Care." Ship your stock so that they will arrive in plenty of time and always pay the express on them, so that there will be no delay whatsoever, and do not forget to put plenty of food to last your cavies enroute. Feed your show stock cautiously and give them plenty of food which contains good nourishment.

GROOMING CAVIES—It is an important thing to comb and get the coat of the cavy in the best of condition. Any cavy can be improved by sufficient grooming, and we will say a few words in regard to the smooth haired cavy: If you will rub your hand over the cavy a great number of times you will find that the coat will continue to become smooth, and this, of course, has a great deal to do in attracting the attention of the judge. Some use a chamois, although a silk handkerchief is very good in preparing cavy coats.

PREPARING ABYSSINIANS.—Long-haired varieties require little different treatment: You should select your best youngsters, which have the most rosettes, and each day take them out of the hutch and stroke out the rosettes with the finger. This will make them form in better shape and also will cause the cavy not to become frightened and to sit comfortably in the palm of your hand at any time. This is an advantage to the judge in judging them. It is not a good thing to show young cavies until they are about three months old. Grown cavies should be handled practically the same as the youngsters. Never mind the appearance of the rosettes

PROFIT IN GUINEA PIGS

of the animals, for they are perfectly natural and no one can produce them differently. If you are showing solid color varieties and you have one or two faulty hairs about the stock that are not desirable, it is well to pluck them out. Of course, there are a great many tricks in regard to showing cavies. However, a good judge most always notices them and takes them into consideration.

PREPARING PERUVIAN CAVIES.—The Peruvians are the hardest cavies to care for and require a great deal of attention in getting them ready for the show, because of the length of hair which they carry. You should thoroughly and carefully brush their coat and keep it from entangling, and the brushing will also bring out the brilliance of the fur. They should be combed each day, starting about a month before show time, and keep them in clean dry hutches, and it is well to keep each Peruvian in a separate hutch before the show, if not they will bite the hair off each other.

We have mentioned how cavies should be shipped to the show, and if you desire to sell any stock during the show and you are unable to be there, it is well to take the matter up with the secretary and advise him what your price is on each animal. They generally charge 10% of the amount of the sale as the expense money in selling your stock. Association shows always charge an entry fee, which generally amounts to about 50 cents for each cavy exhibited. Display pens are also charged for according to the number and size that you wish. Express is paid by the exhibitor, and generally the association furnishes feed for the stock without charge to the exhibitor, and they also furnish a man in charge who will take care of the stock and see that it is properly handled, fed and shipped.

Exhibition cavies are generally entered as senior female and senior male, junior female and junior male,

PROFIT IN GUINEA PIGS

and this pertains to all classes. Stock should not be entered under four months old in the senior class, and no stock entered over four months old in the junior class.

There are various premiums given by the different associations. Some in the form of ribbons, money and cups.

CAVY BREEDERS' ASSOCIATION

Every person engaged in the Cavy industry should by all means, as a benefit to her or himself, contribute to the support of this association by sending their name and one dollar yearly dues to the Secretary.

We are doing everything in our power, with our available means, to assist the raiser of cavies to broaden or increase his profits, to establish friendly relations and feelings among our members, and the Cavy breeders in general. We are sanctioning large Cavy shows and working for more of them. At these shows we place special cash awards for our members.

We are fighting the express rates and hope soon to have them reduced to a single first-class rate. We are boosting the Cavy as a food product and the beautiful hide as a commercial fur.

We will soon start issuing a quarterly bulletin (free to members) to keep them posted on the working, progress, etc., of the association as well as what is doing in a general way in the Cavy world. With a large membership at present, and our growth continuing, we hope by January 1st, 1923, to have over 2,000 members. Think what can be accomplished with this money and the coöperation of this number of active members. Our officers receive no financial compensation for their continual labor for the benefit of the Cavy industry, and fancy, we receive our rewards through the good work we have been able to accomplish with the splendid sup-

PROFIT IN GUINEA PIGS

port and coöperation our members have and are extending to us and OUR and YOUR association. We are anxious and always glad to receive advice and suggestions from our members, and are always willing to help them whenever possible.

As a little illustration of the work we are doing, will cite the Cavy Show held at Pueblo in connection with the Colorado State Fair. The Western Cavy Breeders' Association sanctioned this show. One of our members, Mr. Karl M. Frey, of Pueblo, was appointed Superintendent of the Cavy Department.

All stock was exhibited in uniform wire cooping, single deck. Over $400.00 was paid in cash prizes, and in addition many handsome silver cups, trophies and merchandise specials were awarded. The total number of Cavies on exhibition ran close to the 500 mark. One exhibitor showed 246 head. This entire exhibit (246) was sold at the show and shipped from the showroom direct to the purchaser.

This show broke three records:

First, being the largest Cavy show ever held in the United States.

Second, the largest exhibit by one exhibitor at a show.

Third, the largest cash premium awards ever awarded at a Cavy show.

This coming season we will hold many sanctioned shows and hope to break more records, and are anxious to see how "BIG" we can really get, what good we can do and how many we can help and how many we can get to help others.

In conclusion, will say that the Western Cavy Breeders' Association is proud of its achievements, proud of its members and proud of its name. It is the one and only real Guinea Pig Missionary Society in action today. We will surely appreciate your aid, coöperation and membership, for which—we thank you.

Ailments of Cavies

CAVIES are really not subject to many diseases. Their susceptibility to ailment is closely related to quality, quantity and kind of food eaten. Feeding cavies at irregular times and in improper amounts are generally the sources of the common causes of inflammation affecting the stomach digestive tract, from which losses among the animals may occur. Too sudden changes in temperature in localities where the freezing point varies considerably and also having insufficient and improper ventilation are common causes of pneumonia. Direct drafts will also cause this disease. If you will take due precautions as to feeding, cleanliness of surroundings, pure water, abundant room and reasonably even temperature and proper ventilation, you will prevent almost any of the diseases cavies are subject to. Some authorities state that cavies are practically immune from disease; however, this is not correct. In caring for your cavies, they should not be subject to wet hutches or dampness, which is generally the common cause of fatalities among the cavies. The following diseases as listed, with their symptoms and treatments, will be of great service in caring for the ailments of the cavies if followed carefully.

Colds and Pneumonia. Symptoms: Cavy breathes fast, sides work in and out, hair stands up, animal is in dumpish condition and sits in the corner of the hutch, eats but little. You can generally detect a cavy well developed with this disease by mucus rails obstructing the breathing of the animal, which causes a slight roaring.

Causes: Caused from drafts, sudden change in temperature, overfeeding of green food and keeping them in

PROFIT IN GUINEA PIGS

wet hutches. Sometimes contracted by cavies being placed in a crowded express car and express piled on top of the boxes they are shipped in, causing the cavies to sweat and become overheated. In this condition they are placed in cold express offices where there is considerable draft. Cavies will contract an acute cold in six hours, which generally kills them inside of twelve hours. However, if they pass over the acute condition, which is up to twelve hours, then they pass into the chronic stage, and they will prolong a considerable time, either showing improvement or death.

Treatment: Separate sick cavies from the healthy stock. Give one teaspoonful of castor oil at night after feeding. Begin next morning with one drop aconite, placing in cavy's mouth with dropper morning and evening until cured. Cut down on green food one-half.

Crooked Neck or Tortocolis. Symptoms: The animal holds head to one side and goes around in a circle.

Causes: Caused by drafts and catching cold, which affects the muscles of the neck, causing the muscles which is affected most to give the neck a curved appearance. Some animals recover from this. Although their neck is turned, they make very good breeders.

Treatment: Massage the neck of the animal with any good liniment and give three drops of sweet spirits of nitre night and morning. This generally relieves them and often cures.

Watery Eyes. Symptoms: Watery discharge from the eyes and sometimes from the nostrils, caused by a cold and sometimes the ammonia given off from unclean hutches. If caused from colds follow the same treatment as for colds and pneumonia.

Paralysis. Symptoms: Hind quarters drag, weak backs, lower extremities of cavy immovable.

PROFIT IN GUINEA PIGS

Caused from feeding too much alfalfa or overfeeding them with green food; also damp hutches.

Treatment: Give cavy 20 drops of sweet spirits of nitre twice a day. Rub the limbs and loin with some good liniment. Feed carefully for a few days and they will generally recover.

Abscesses. Symptoms: Bunches form around the throat of the cavy, or perhaps on its back. This is caused by an overheated condition of the blood affecting the glands.

Treatment: When the abscess is ripe and in a softened condition, clip the hair from around same and lance the abscess with a knife. Squeeze out the pus and wash surrounding parts with a good disinfectant and use a piece of cotton on a match dipped in iodine and swab cavity thoroughly. You can prevent these abscesses by feeding a sulphur tonic to your cavies.

Premature Birth. Cavies born dead or born so weak that they do not live long. Sometimes the mother cavy may die also. This is most always caused by too much handling, by fright, falling, over-fatness or physical weakness.

Treatment: Watch your cavies when they become heavy and ready to have young. If they are too crowded in the hutches, separate them. If you think they are too fat, cut down on the feed. Above all, do not handle your cavies when they are heavy. If you want to separate them from one hutch to another, you should have the cavies walk onto a tray and move tray and all to the new quarters.

Lice. Symptoms: Animals become thin, do not seem to eat, scratch themselves considerably; hair sometimes stands up and the cavy has sort of a dull appearance. Always look your cavy over about once or twice a month for nits and lice, for these pests hinder the growth and breeding of stock and keep them in a poor condition.

Treatment: If the weather is warm, it is well that you dip them, and you can generally get an animal dip that is prepared especially for this, as per directions from the manufacturer. You can dip the entire animal in the fluid and place them in the sun where it is warm so that they will dry rapidly, or near a stove if you wish. Dipping cavies is really the sure way of destroying lice. However, if the weather is too cold for dipping, then use a good lice powder and dust same into the hair of the cavy and about the hutch. Do not be afraid of using too much.

Diarrhoea. Symptoms: Animal discharges watery substance and gradually gets thin and will not eat, caused by too much green food, mouldy and half-cured hay. A sudden change of food is usually the cause.

Treatment: Give them plenty of good sweet hay and omit the green food for a time, and give them one teaspoonful of castor oil to eliminate the cause and feed them on dry food until improved.

Broken Teeth. Sometimes cavies will fight in their hutches and cause their teeth to be broken. This is very bad for the animal, because it is necessary that you feed them soft food until their teeth have grown out. In showing stock it is a very important thing that your cavies have good teeth, as it is hard to condition an animal unless they can chew and digest their food properly.

Blindness. Symptoms: Cavies have small white spots form on the eyeball. This is due to running straws into their eyes or sometimes from the poor condition of the blood. Many cavies shortly after they are born fail to open the lids of their eyes, caused from the lids becoming stuck together. It is well for you to watch your young stock so you can avoid blindness and spread the lids of the cavy's eyes open.

Treatment: A few drops of rose water and boracic acid mixed together is very good for clearing the pupil of the eye.

Diseases of the Skin. Symptoms: Cavy loses hair in patches. On examination you will note little scurf on the surface. Animal sits around in hutch and does not move a great deal on account of soreness.

Treatment: Dipping as mentioned above for lice is the best treatment, for a good disinfectant will destroy it in one dipping; however, you can use any good sulphur ointment, or ask for Fowler's Solution at the drug store, which is also very effective.

Mickey Weaning Out the Young When They Are Three Weeks Old. Laboratory Stock.

Summary

DO you know of any industry that you can enter into with less capital, less work and less worry, and yet show almost immediate results than the raising of guinea pigs, which is an outdoor enterprise and one that does not require all of your time, depending, of course, on the number of stock you have. For instance, a person can care for 2500 breeders nicely by devoting his entire time to same. This will give you an idea of division of time in comparison to the number that you can care for.

Many people, who are along in years, find this a most fascinating proposition, and one that they enjoy, because it does not confine them to indoor work. Numerous young people who are not so certain of a future enter into the raising of Cavies, and locate on small acreage where they enjoy the living conditions, which are great deal better than they could secure in the city, financially and otherwise.

The Cavy development of the past has advanced very rapidly, and a great many people are entering the field each year. The field is large and the demand for cavies is steadily growing.

Many women throughout the United States are now large raisers. The fancy has developed as much as the animal has been improved. The goal the breeders are working for today is a state of perfection and symmetry, as those points appeal to the critic's eye. Numerous breeders are adhering to a certain type or variety, spending their time in bringing this particular variety up to perfection, and in that way demand higher prices for their quality of stock. Breeding exper-

PROFIT IN GUINEA PIGS

iments have been tried for years, and success came as a result. Consequently, there are hundreds of people, all classes and ages, who have gathered together and organized Cavy Clubs and Associations for the purpose of breeding and exhibiting better Cavies.

Several notable women have established Caviaries and take a great deal of pride in their stock and exhibit them at the different Cavy shows. Competition is becoming keen at the Cavy shows, and it takes a mighty good animal to win nowadays if there are more than five in a class, as the animal shows off well for the reason that they do not bite or scratch, and make very interesting pets. The long haired Peruvians, when properly groomed, make a beautiful sight, as their long, flowing hair is glossy and smooth as silk, and the animal itself gives the appearance of a fur muff, for its long hair covers its head and feet as well as the body.

Movie stars and professional people carry the Peruvian Cavies in preference to Pomeranian dogs.

The newspapers throughout the country often take up the topic of Cavies and have published various articles in regard to them, which has done a great deal to the advancement of the Cavy industry.

The Cavy is looked upon today as an animal returning large profits, and the day of raising Cavies as a hobby and pastime is passing, as people are taking it up as a business proposition for the benefit of all concerned. Cavies are claimed by some to be the fastest breeding and most thriving animal known if properly cared for. For the majority of animals classed under "Live Stock," it takes a considerable length of time to produce offspring and many months' time and money spent in growing them until they become useful. However, the Cavy is quite different—to our advantage—because they can be bred at the age of two months or so, and generally have

PROFIT IN GUINEA PIGS

young when they are four and one-half or five months old.

As a rule, animals are of considerable expense in raising before they get to the age when they will return a profit, but the Cavies are small and require very little feed, time and space. It is not necessary to have the spacious runs and kennel accommodations that are necessary for other animals. If you are raising dogs it entails an expenditure on maintenance and veterinary skill far beyond the reach of the pockets of many. Poultry come under the same head. Rabbits are detrimental to sanitation if kept in the ordinary back yard. There are no objections to Cavies, if their hutches are cleaned once a week.

It would be well for you to attend a Cavy Show and see the enthusiastic breeders talking the various varieties and the great interest shown at the judging bench when the stock is passed upon as to merits, etc., for here is where they undergo the keenest criticism.

The sportsmanship in breeding and showing Cavies is the genuiness of their enthusiasm, and once you become infected with the germ, you will be an enthusiast forever.

We believe that you will agree with us, after carefully reading this book, that there is no other industry or occupation that can be started with so little expenditure of money, time or space, and at the same time that produces such good returns, as the raising of guinea pigs. Even a few pens properly cared for will not only furnish an abundance of pleasure and amusement, but will also be the source of a modern income, while if the business is conducted on a larger scale there is no limit to production and your profits will be just what you choose to make them.

Guinea Pigs are more easily and more economically raised than any other domestic animal, and require less

PROFIT IN GUINEA PIGS

room, less housing and less food. Their hutches can be quickly and cheaply made from ordinary packing boxes, while they thrive and develop rapidly on the simplest and cheapest of food. They are very healthy and hardy, do well in any climate, are clean in their habits and have no disagreeable odor as most other animals have. These pleasing characteristics make them popular as pets and caring for them is a delight not only to boys and girls but to grown-ups as well.

Guinea Pigs—or Cavies, as they are most correctly called—are native to South America and in their wild state are a trifle smaller than the domesticated animals and are of a rusty, grayish-brown color. Where the name "pig" originated or became connected with the Cavy is not thoroughly understood, as the Guinea Pig does not resemble pigs in any way, size, shape or habits, but are more like a rabbit in shape and habits, except that they have very short legs, short, rounded ears and no tail. They feed upon nearly all vegetable substances, but drink very little water.

None of the domestic animals or pets are more prolific than the Guinea Pig. They begin to breed at from two to three months of age and can average four litters a year, as a rule. The number of young to the litter is from two to six, but three may be considered as the average. The little fellows are born fully furred with eyes open. In a few hours they are able to eat the same food as the mother, and in ten days or three weeks may be weaned entirely.

Guinea Pigs are members of the rodent family, as are squirrels, rabbits, etc., and their diet is entirely vegetarian. In summer time there is practically no expense to their feed, as they will grow rapidly on lawn clippings, dandelions, green cornstalks, or fresh vegetables such as carrots, beets or cabbages. In winter they are very fond of hay of any kind, also oats, bran, shorts and

PROFIT IN GUINEA PIGS

other similar grain products. Table scraps, dry bread, etc., help to fill out an inexpensive ration. This small cost of feeding should have favorable consideration compared with the cost of food for poultry, rabbits, or other domestic animals, and is one of the reasons why the raising of Guinea Pigs is so profitable.

In their wild state, Cavies live in burrows, among the crevices of rocks or beneath the large leaves of plants in marshy places. The domestic Guinea Pigs will live and thrive in most any kind of inclosure, provided they are protected from cold draughts and wet weather. They should also be protected from dogs, cats and rats.

Because of their adaptability to most any climate or condition, Guinea Pigs may be successfully raised by any one and anywhere. They do equally well in the North where the temperature may drop to zero or below, and in the South where cold weather is unknown. The barn, the city back yard, a dry, well-lighted cellar or a spare room in the house, all are suitable places to raise Guinea Pigs. If kept in the house as pets, they are no more offensive than cats, dogs, or canary birds.

There are several varieties of Guinea Pigs, but the ones most generally used and for which there is the greatest demand, are the English or smooth haired Guinea Pigs, the kind that is most profitable to raise. They grow very rapidly and should weigh from eight to twelve ounces at the age of one month or six weeks, and when fully matured weigh about two pounds or more. The colors are white, black, red, cream and mixed. The solid colors, of course, denote purer and more careful breeding and are preferred by some raisers, while others may prefer the mixed colors. Like cattle, the best markings show the best breeding.

Cavies are very popular in England, and we hope the United States will take as great an interest in Cavies as they have there. No show of stock in the foreign

PROFIT IN GUINEA PIGS

countries is complete without an exhibition of Cavies of all varieties.

A great many noted breeders in England have put forth great efforts in promoting the Cavy. Mr. George Gardner and Mr. C. A. House have written several books on Cavies, and as good books on Cavies give you the various ideas on this industry, it would be well for you to secure copies, for there has not been many books written on this subject. Other breeders who deserve a great deal of credit in improving and breeding stock are Mr. J. Walker, Mr. G. Billet, Mr. Alf. Outhwaite, Mr. H. H. Brown and Mr. A. Roberts.

A few years ago the United States Department of Agriculture issued a bulletin, "Farmers' Bulletin No. 525," called "Raising Guinea Pigs," which has been revised from time to time, for the purpose of interesting the public in this proposition, which we quote below:

"Raising guinea pigs, or cavies, requires no extraordinary knowledge and no great outlay of capital. The animals are hardy, aside from being susceptible to cold. They are easily managed, and little space is needed to accommodate them. They make interesting pets and are useful as food animals and for scientific purposes. Medical research and other scientific investigations have created a demand for them which should insure remunerative prices to those who are favorably located. It is not advisable to breed cavies in large numbers without first being assured of a market. Profit in breeding the animals for scientific purposes is largely dependent on an opportunity of selling them promptly when they are from 6 to 8 weeks old.

"This bulletin gives brief but plain directions for the management of guinea pigs. Since it was first published, in 1913, many persons have engaged in raising the animals for laboratory uses, and increased produc-

PROFIT IN GUINEA PIGS

tion has tended to lower the prices. Importations have practically ceased. Production of cavies for exhibition and food purposes and for pets has increased, also, and many persons are breeding them solely as fancy stock.

"Numerous inquiries received by the Department of Agriculture concerning proper methods of raising guinea pigs, or cavies, show a widespread interest in the subject throughout the United States. A few years ago when the demand for guinea pigs for laboratory purposes was great the animals were very difficult to obtain, and, because of the lack of production in this country, few were to be had. As a result, large numbers were imported. Importations have now practically ceased, but applications for information on breeding the animals continue, as they have a food value and are useful for experimental and other purposes.

"Guinea pigs are raised chiefly as pets or fancy stock and for scientific purposes. The instructions herein given are applicable to either. These are based mainly on the experience of the Bureau of Animal Industry, which has generously allowed the use of the results of its experiments in the preparation of this paper. For several years that bureau has raised large numbers of guinea pigs in its investigations of heredity and the effects of inbreeding, as well as for laboratory uses. The methods employed have been uniformly successful at both of its breeding establishments near Washington.

"The cost of raising a guinea pig to maturity (age 4 or 5 months) at the department stations has been estimated by those in charge at from 50 to 60 cents. With their own labor, private breeders, especially farmers with plenty of green food at command, can reduce the cost by half.

"In medical research, especially in testing and standardizing antitoxins, immature animals weighing 250

PROFIT IN GUINEA PIGS

grams (nearly 9 ounces) are required. This weight is attained in about six weeks, and the cost of feeding the animals until suitable for this purpose will be correspondingly less. They sell at various prices, dependent on supply and demand. The average for several years has been about 75 cents. When this bulletin was first published (1913) the animals were scarce, and laboratories paid as high as $1.00 to $1.50 each for their supply. Increased production in America has since lowered the prices considerably and the average paid in 1921 was from 50 to 60 cents an animal. Even at this low price, persons who are favorably situated near cities or institutions requiring large numbers of guinea pigs may be able to establish a profitable business in supplying the animals. Aside from laboratory uses, there is a growing demand for them as fancy and pet stock.

WILD CAVIES

"Guinea pigs belong to a family of rodents known as the Cavidae, characterized by stout bodies, short incisor teeth, uncleft upper lip, nearly equal legs, and short or rudimentary tails. The front feet are four-toed, and hind ones three-toed. The family is exclusively South American and includes, besides the true Cavies, two other living genera, the maras (Patagonian cavies) and the capybara. All are rather closely allied in structure to the rabbits, and in their native habitats are hunted as game. About 20 species and races of true cavies have been described. Unlike the domestic cavy, or guinea pig, they all have constant colors and breed but once or twice a year.

THE DOMESTIC CAVY

"Of the origin of the domestic cavy little is known. When the Spaniards first invaded the Andean region of South America the animal was found domesticated and

PROFIT IN GUINEA PIGS

living in large numbers in the houses of the Indians, by whom it was used for food. The cavy was carried to Europe by Dutch traders during the sixteenth century. Since then it has been kept in the Old World and in North America chiefly as a pet, and until recently has been generally regarded as an animal of little practical utility. The name "Pig" is readily suggested by its form, but the origin of "guinea" as applied to it is unknown, but may be a corruption of "Guiana pig."

GUINEA PIGS AS PETS

"For four centuries the guinea pig was regarded merely as a pet and bred for show and fancy alone. Being a plastic animal, it was considerably changed during this period, and several strains and modifications of the original were developed. Thus, besides the smooth haired forms, we have the Peruvian, which is a very long-haired type, and the Abyssinian, a type with rather long hair standing out in curious rosettes all over the body.

"The long-haired cavies are not recommended for ordinary pets, as their coats need much care. The smooth-haired require less attention and make equally attractive pets. They have the advantages of being easily kept and of never biting when handled. However, it is not advisable to subject pet animals of any sort to much handling or fondling. Even dogs and cats are always the worse for such treatment, and pet rabbits or guinea pigs soon show the results of much handling in their roughened coats and lack of sprightliness. Long-haired guinea pigs, especially if intended for show, require some handling, since the hair has to be brushed frequently. This is best done while the animal rests on a high shelf, where it need not be held during the brushing.

PROFIT IN GUINEA PIGS

GUINEA PIGS AS FOOD

"It is difficult to account for the somewhat prevalent notion that no rodents are fit for human food. Because of such prejudice, some people will not eat rabbits or squirrels, and probably many others are kept from eating such excellent game as muskrats and prairie dogs. While guinea pigs are seldom eaten in the United States, their near relationship to rabbits and the fact that they are wholly vegetarian in habit should reassure any one who may entertain doubts about their fitness for the table. All the species of wild cavies are accounted good game in South America. Rock cavies, especially, are much hunted in parts of Brazil. Probably the small size of the domestic species is the chief cause for its neglect as a food animal, yet we have other highly esteemed game animals that furnish less meat than a guinea pig.

"The Peruvian method of dressing the guinea pig for cooking is the one generally adopted wherever it is eaten. The animal is killed by dislocating its neck, after which it goes through about the same processes as a suckling pig in preparation for cooking. Its throat is cut, it is hung up for a few minutes to bleed, and is then scalded in water, not too hot at first. The hair is removed, the skin scraped with a knife, the viscera taken out, and the carcass washed in tepid water. It is then ready to cook. The Peruvians usually roast the animals, but the number of possible ways of cooking them is unlimited. Charles Cumberland states that they are excellent eating when cooked in any of the ways that are applied to small game. They may be baked whole, or may be cut into pieces and fried or fricasseed. Says Cumberland:

"'Cavies are excellent as entrees in various stews— with mushrooms, with brown onions, with green peas, a la soubise, and especially in a curry. A practical cook will have no difficulty in varying the preparations, and I will undertake to say that it will be found difficult to make them other than "very good meate."'

"On account of the whiteness of its skin the smooth-haired white (albino) guinea pig is best adapted for the table. The males become somewhat strong flavored with age, but are fine when 4 or 5 months old. Females are tender and finely flavored for a much longer time. They are probably at their best when about a year old.

SCIENTIFIC USE FOR GUINEA PIGS

"Guinea pigs are in much demand for experimental uses in the preparation, testing and standardizing of serums and antitoxins. They are well adapted for this purpose, being small and easily handled. Their use in medical research is steadily increasing, and some of the larger institutions, unable to secure a steady supply of reliable stock for their purposes, have set up breeding establishments of their own.

"Sometimes guinea pigs found in bird stores are unfit for laboratory experiments. They may have been previously used for serum or antitoxin tests or may be the offspring of animals that have survived such tests. Unless the dealer knows the source from which the animals came and can absolutely guarantee that they have never been used for experiments, he can rarely sell them to institutions. Any breeder undertaking to supply animals to laboratories must give absolute assurance as to their suitability for experiments. If he can do this and furnish the animals as needed, he should be able to command good prices for them and to establish a permanent and lucrative business.

MANAGEMENT OF GUINEA PIGS

"Few animals are as easily raised as guinea pigs. They are much less subject to disease than rabbits. The more important items in their management will be explained under the headings: Selection of Stock; Hutches and Pens; Feed and Feeding; Breeding, and Diseases and Enemies.

SELECTION OF STOCK

"Except for show purposes the only kind of guinea pigs that should be grown are the smooth-haired varieties. These are of several colors. Those with pink eyes are albinos, usually pure white but sometimes more or less marked with obscure spots. Occasionally an individual guinea pig is of a single color other than white. Thus it may be red, gray, brown, or glossy black, but it seems difficult to maintain a pure strain of 'selfs' except the white. The majority of domestic cavies are spotted, the common colors being fawn, light gray, red-brown, dark brown, and cream, interspersed with white or black or both white and black. The pigment of the hair usually corresponds to that of the skin, which is white only under white or cream areas of fur.

"If guinea pigs are raised for table use, light-colored kinds are to be preferred; if for scientific purposes, color is of little importance, although distinctive markings are desirable. When raised for pets or for show, the fancy of the breeder may be followed. In any case strong, healthy animals of good size should be chosen for breeding stock. A full-grown cavy in good flesh should weigh nearly two pounds. This weight will not often be attained under 18 months of age. Instances of 3 pounds weight for males at 3 years have been recorded. As a rule, females, except when pregnant, are lighter than males of the same age. The chief point in selecting stock is to obtain healthy animals that will mature quickly and attain a good size.

HUTCHES AND PENS

(See Article—"Housing of Cavies," by Government.)

FEED AND FEEDING

"Guinea pigs require about the same diet as rabbits. They eat frequently during the day and need a constant supply of staple dry feed. Three articles should be constantly in each hutch or run—a pan of water supplied fresh at least once a day, a piece of rock salt, and a pan for dry grain, which may contain oats, bran or chopped grain. The animals should also have a constant supply of hay, of which they eat large quantities, and a daily feed of green stuff. They eat almost every kind of green food that is relished by rabbits—cabbage, celery tops, and lettuce are especially acceptable, but fresh cut alfalfa and clover, spinach, kale, rape, and the like are also desirable green foods. For winter it is best to have a good supply of cabbages. These may be stored in the field, covered with leaves or straw, with a layer of soil on top, and may be brought in as wanted, so that they do not need to be fed in wilted condition. With a plentiful supply of green feed, guinea pigs drink but little water, yet it is well to have water always at hand for them. In the absence of green feed, water becomes an absolute necessity, as these animals refuse to eat grain without it.

BREEDING

"Guinea pigs breed at a very early age. The females are sexually matured when about a month old, but should not be allowed to breed so early.

"The fecundity of guinea pigs has been greatly exaggerated. Buffon states that they breed every six weeks and commonly have litters of 12 each. This error has been republished from time to time until it seems to have become fixed in the popular mind. As a matter of fact, many other rodents are far more prolific. The female guinea pig has but two teats, and her period of

PROFIT IN GUINEA PIGS

gestation varies from 63 to 70 days. Ordinarily five litters may be expected in a year, averaging about three young each. The first litter produced by a female usually consists of but 1 or 2. Subsequent ones are commonly larger, but they rarely number more than 5 or 6. A female in her breeding prime may be expected to raise about 12 to 15 young each year.

"Young guinea pigs are well developed when born, have the eyes open, and are fully furred. They are soon able to run about freely and within a day or two begin to take food other than the mother's milk. When they are about three weeks old the mother ceases to give them attention, but it is better to leave them in the hutch with the parents three or four days longer. The weaned animals should then be placed, each sex by itself, in separate cages. Large hutches accommodating 50 or more of the young are desirable, but it is not well to keep males of different sizes in the same cage, as the stronger are apt to fight and injure the weaker ones.

"When 5 or 6 months old the young females may be distributed to breeding pens. From 3 to 5 should be kept permanently with one male; but the best results will probably be attained with the smaller number, since the young when newly born will be in less danger from overcrowding. The males should be chosen from among animals older than the young females. Inbreeding is not considered harmful unless continued for eight or ten generations. Usually the females agree well together, and when two have young at about the same time both nurse the progeny indiscriminately. Occasionally two females are antagonistic, and then it is desirable to separate them.

"The hutches should be thoroughly cleaned twice a week and fresh litter supplied for the floors. Oat straw, chaff, fine hay, and sawdust all make excellent bedding. It is not necessary to remove or handle the animals while cleaning the hutches, but this should be done when it is desired to fumigate either hutches or runs.

DISEASES AND ENEMIES

"As already stated, guinea pigs are not subject to many diseases. Their susceptibility to ailments is closely related to the quality, quantity, and kind of food eaten. Improper, irregular, and deficient feeding are common causes of inflammation of the stomach and bowels, from which losses among the animals may be very great. Sudden changes of temperature, particularly downward to the freezing point, and insufficient and improper ventilation, are common causes of pneumonia, which is extremely fatal among guinea pigs. Bountiful and judicious feeding, cleanliness of surroundings, pure water, abundant room, reasonably constant temperature, and proper ventilation are almost certain preventatives of disease. The coats of guinea pigs should not be allowed to become wet, and the hutches should be carefully guarded against dampness, which is a common cause of fatalities among the animals.

"The chief enemy of the guinea pig is the common rat. This pest is popularly supposed to avoid premises where guinea pigs are kept. On the contrary, it is attracted by the grain fed, and will not only steal the food of the cavies, but has been known to gnaw through the hutch walls and devour the young. The extermination of rats after they have thoroughly established themselves about the premises is no easy task. Preventative measures are usually much more effective. In a neighborhood that is rat infested, buildings intended for housing guinea pigs should be made rat proof."

PROFIT IN GUINEA PIGS

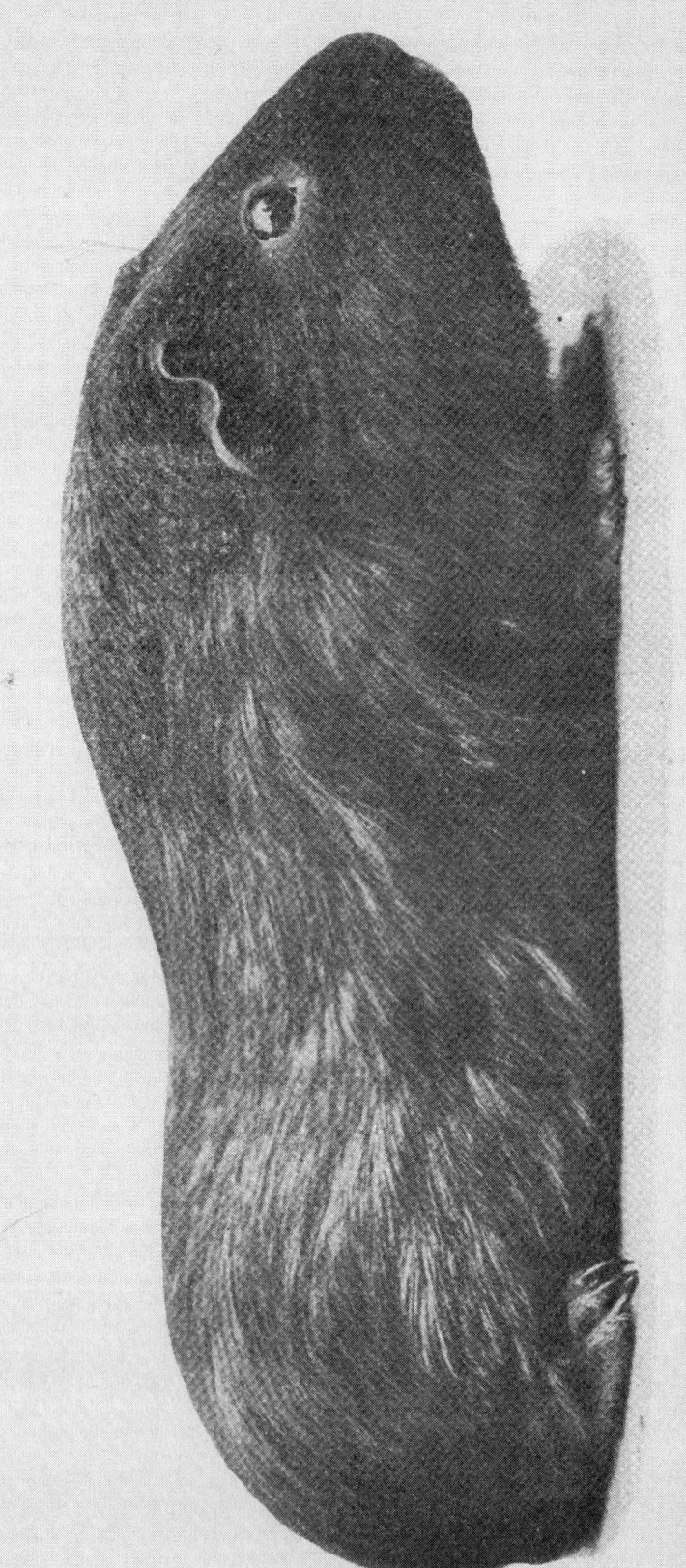

A perfect smooth Red English male. Note the bright round eye, well drooped ear, rotund of shoulder, clear shaped head and nose, characteristic conformation.

# Special Articles

Meat and Fur Production

By E. D. Wheeler,

Secretary, Western Cavy Breeders' Association,

1315 W. Cucharras St., Colorado Springs, Colo.

Shall embody in the following article my actual experience in breeding cavies on a large commercial scale. This will be of great benefit to the beginner and will also be interesting to the experienced breeder.

During the fifteen years I have been engaged in the raising of guinea pigs, will say that at no time have I had less than three hundred breeders on hand, and often as high as thirty-five hundred.

Have kept an accurate account of all receipts and expenditures, and the results are amazing in regard to the wonderful profits received from the stock. The demand for cavies has developed so fast in late years that I am compelled to return many orders for stock on account of the extreme shortage of cavies.

I have experimented with all varieties, and have ran yearly tests to prove exactly what could be accomplished along different ideas and conditions.

I have raised forty-nine pigs from one pair of cavies in one year. You can therefore see the remarkable production of these little animals. I placed 100 females (50 virgin and 50 tried breeders) in 20 pens (5 in each pen), and in each pen placed one male, and in one year these one hundred females had 1,207 young. Females in the young greatly predominated.

PROFIT IN GUINEA PIGS

Guinea pigs are not unlike other stock when ready to market. We find at times the large cattle and hog raisers are reluctant to sell their stock on account of market conditions at certain times. Prices of stock fluctuate to some extent. It was during a time that prices were low that I found myself possessed of a large number of males—large ones that could not be delivered profitably on a ten-ounce contract. My solution of this

MR. E. D. WHEELER
Secy. Western Cavy Breeders' Assn.

problem was to interest several clubs and restaurants in cavy meat as a table food and as a result I am now regularly supplying several customers with dressed cavies, and the demand is rapidly increasing.

Their beautiful skins are in big demand, and when made into gloves, auto robes, fur garments, etc., bring

PROFIT IN GUINEA PIGS

handsome prices. The tendency of the user of guinea pigs is to contract with a large breeder or dealer for his regular supply, and until a small raiser can equip himself with sufficient breeders to insure his output large enough to get in the field in open competition it is best that he should make arrangements with some reliable dealer to handle his surplus. The first thing to do is to dress several males one-half to two-thirds grown. Fry them like you would a spring chicken, young rabbit or quail, and proceed to feast yourself thereon. Will venture to say that after you do this you will not be trying to dispose of a few odd males, but you will be a booster for cavy meat and you will see the future possibilities of the cavy industry. You will increase your number of breeders and enlarge your plant, just as others are doing after proving to their own satisfaction by practical experiments and tests of the most rigid nature that "THERE IS MONEY IN CAVIES."

You Will Note Cavies Do Not Take Up a Great Deal of Space

PROFIT IN GUINEA PIGS

Breeding Show Cavies

By E. D. CORRIN
President of Western Cavy Breeders' Association.

A few words of advice and some timely suggestions from an experienced cavy breeder. Every one should read them, for they contain something of value to all.

Before commencing to get together your breeding stock, the beginner should carefully study the show

E. D. CORRIN
President of Western Cavy Breeders' Association
Colorado Springs, Colo.

PROFIT IN GUINEA PIGS

reports in our fancier papers to see who are the successful breeders on the show bench and have stock for sale.

Having done this, the next thing to do is to decide which variety he wants to take up. In deciding on the variety, space, time and cash at disposal must be considered. The room required for 20 English will only accommodate 10 Peruvians. The time required to look after Peruvians is much greater than that needed to care for a stud of English. The question of variety being settled, the novice should place himself in communication with some of our best breeders. Most of our leading fanciers may be depended upon. All leading breeders and exhibitors have a reputation to uphold and invariably are willing to do their best to help the new beginner who asks their assistance in the selection of their stock.

Should a novice go to an experienced fancier and pretend that he knows all about cavies, he will make a mistake. A conceited, know-it-all novice is almost certain to get fooled. In selecting stock a great point is the perfect healthfulness of each one selected. The future success of a caviary depends in a great measure on the healthfulness of the original stock. It is impossible to breed exhibition stock from unhealthy parents. All that you can do is to propagate disease and eventually death. A good test as to health and vigor is the condition of the eye and coat. A cavy in good health is sleek and glossy in coat, while the eyes are bold, bright and glistening. A healthy cavy is active and fast in its movements. An unhealthy cavy is dull in eye, open in coat and is slow and dull in its movements.

Having selected your cavies, they should be placed in nice, comfortable hutches, free from draughts and dampness, with about two inches of sawdust to absorb the moisture; thus the risks of colds, paralysis, rheumatism, etc., is considerably reduced. One boar and three or

PROFIT IN GUINEA PIGS

four sows may be run together. In selecting sows for breeding you should always give the preference to young sows. It is an acknowledged fact among many of our leading scientific naturalists that the best results in breeding are obtained from young dams. In using young sows, care must be taken to have a boar at least 15 months old or over. This is most important. In regard to the age at which stock should be used for breeding purposes, I am strictly opposed to the use of stock before the age of 7 months at the youngest. If used earlier, the young are not so strong or so finely developed as when bred from matured specimens. Sows that are savage and snap at their owner when he feeds or cleans their pens are not likely to make good mothers. Sulky disposed sows should not be chosen. The best mothers are found among those bright, happy individuals who know their master's step, listen for the sound of his voice, love the stroke of his hand and always greet his coming with joy and gladness, being expressed by their coming to the front of the cage and trying to converse with you in their own language, doing their best to thank you for your attention and care bestowed upon them. Young cavies intended for breeding should be allowed plenty of room for exercise, so that when required for breeding their bodies are well developed and their constitution strong and healthy in every respect. Sows go with young 65 to 70 days. Some a little before and some a little later. Sows that are coming with young should be well fed. Personally, I like to feed soft food during this period: warm mashes composed of one part crushed oats, one part shorts, two parts good broad bran; should be fed every evening. In the morning, good, sound, clean oats with a dish of water or milk should be given them. Toward the close of the pregnancy period, a feed of warm bread and milk should be given every morning. Plenty of green food or roots should be given during the whole period. Carrots are

PROFIT IN GUINEA PIGS

much better than beets at this time; they are sweeter and more conducive to a good milk flow. Breeding sows should never be without liquid or green food in their pens. About a week before you expect young the pens should be cleaned out thoroughly and well bedded with sawdust and hay. The young should run with their mother until five weeks old, and during the whole time they should have bread and milk, night and morning. At this time hay and green food should not be forgotten. A sufficient supply of both should be given twice a day.

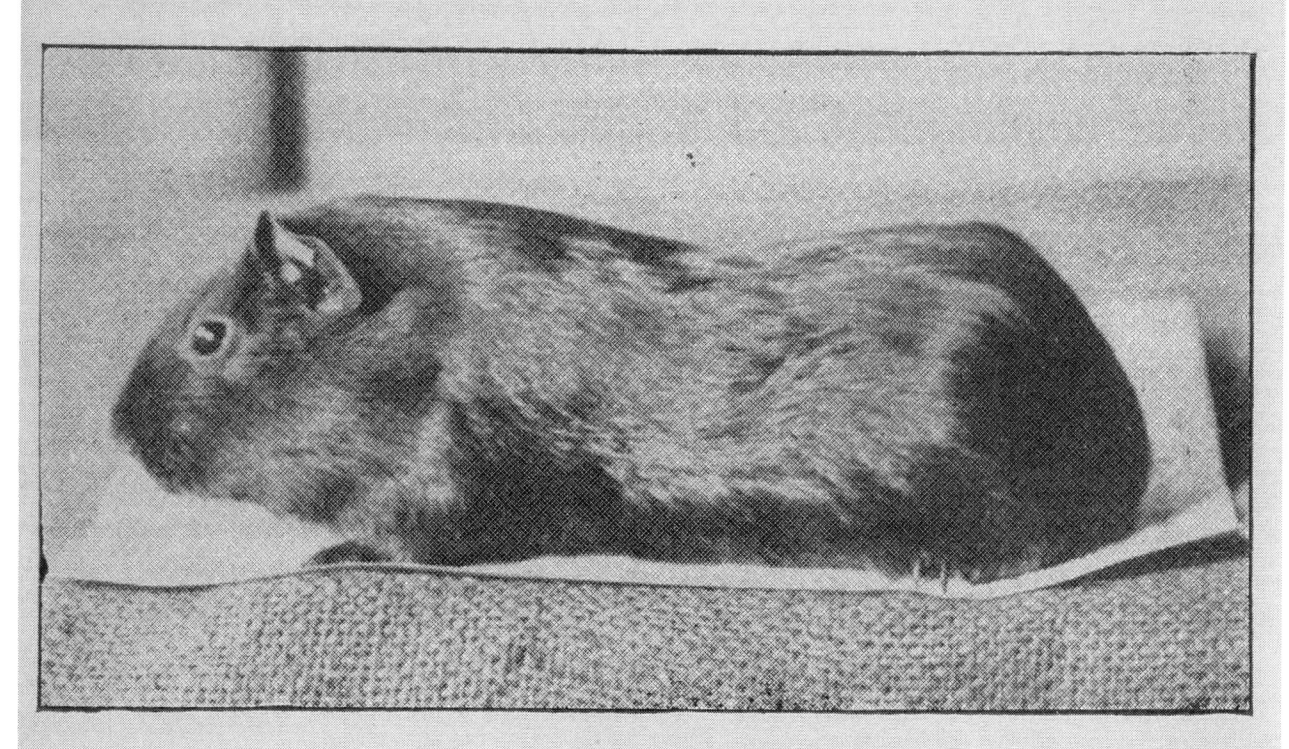

IMPORTED RED ENGLISH SOW
Bred for Quality
Owned by E. D. Corrin

When the young are taken from their mother the sexes should be separated; it is not safe to leave them together after that age. If they are well developed (and they should be) they are very likely to get with young, and if that takes place all your labor to ever raise a good, strong show specimen has been in vain. The individuals that look like developing into winners should be

PROFIT IN GUINEA PIGS

kept separate from ordinary stock and fed on a more luxurious diet, size being a big factor on the show bench.

The young should be pushed as fast as possible from the day of their birth until the date at which they make their "debut" on the show bench.

They should be fed liberally upon bread and milk mashes, good sound oats, hay, carrots and green food. What you put into them at this age will be returned to you when you put them into the breeding pen. Bran contains a large amount of bone-forming matter. The pen should at all times contain clean water. Water is a great preventative of disease. Many diseases are caused through the non-action of the kidneys, carrying all impurities with it, and thus the kidneys are kept healthy and in good working order.

It sometimes happens that a sow does not suckle her young well. This condition may arise from several causes. Should this occur, the young should be transferred to another sow that has recently had young. In moving the young to the foster-mother, you must see that she is a quiet, lovable mother and not liable to harm the little ones committed to her care. Cavies, as a rule, are very good in this way; they have no objection to a stranger or two among their own babies. If a foster-mother is not available, the young must be kept well supplied with new milk, thickened with fine oatmeal.

Although some fanciers run one boar with four or five sows all the time, I think it is not advisable to do so. When the sows are seen to be with young the boar should be removed. As to whether it is best to let the sows remain together is a much-debated point. If the sows are littered together, it might be advantageous to do so, if they are a peaceable bunch. But it sometimes happens that they are not; even some of the best are at this time inclined to be snappy and irritable. When

PROFIT IN GUINEA PIGS

this is the case, trouble naturally follows and in the scramble some of the young are apt to be injured. To avoid this, it is advisable to remove the sows to separate pens a week or so before the young are expected. It is a great advantage, however, to have several sows littering about the same time, for this reason: if one mother goes wrong in any way, her young may be divided among the others; or if one has a large litter and another a small litter, the mothering duties may be divided, to the benefit of all concerned. There has been much argument as to when is the best time to mate sows. One thing is certain: they will more readily respond to the advances of the boar a day or two after they have had their young than at any other time. This, however, seems cruel and unnatural, to say nothing of the exhausting effect it must have on the sows' constitution and loss in size and stamina in her progeny. Personally, I do not believe in such a system of breeding. It is not right that while she is suckling one litter she should be called upon to carry another. Both the born and unborn must naturally suffer, to say nothing of the strain upon the mother.

If, however, she is well fed for four or five weeks after the young are taken from her, she will generally respond to the advances of the boar in a few days from the time of being introduced to him and breed strong, healthy young.

Three litters a year is the most I take from one sow, and oftimes only two. What you don't get in numbers you get in quality. One good one is much better than a dozen poor ones. In all your breeding operations, remember that the great essentials to success are cleanliness, purity of food, regularity in feeding, roomy and well-ventilated pens and the selection of strong, healthy stock. It is useless expecting to become a successful breeder unless these points are well observed. Neglect

PROFIT IN GUINEA PIGS

EDWIN F. DIECKE and DR. J. A. ROBERTS
Judging Cavies

them and failure is sure to overtake you. Observe them and if you do not succeed you will at least have the satisfaction of knowing that failure has not come from any fault of your own. This knowledge will spur you on to greater efforts, and success is bound to sooner or later put you on the list with the fancy breeders. Last, but not least, when you have become a successful breeder and away on top in the show room, do not forget your own struggles and be ever ready to give a helping hand to the new beginner, for you must always bear in mind that the novice is the backbone of the industry, and you will be long remembered in the fancy class after your own activities have ceased as a true fancier and a gentleman.

PROFIT IN GUINEA PIGS

Judging English Show Cavies

(By JUDGE LEWIS S. J. GRIFFIN.)
Colorado Springs, Colorado

I will state briefly a few points, mainly how a judge places awards on English cavies; also what constitutes the principal points to be considered. In dealing with the judge's point of view, one must imagine himself now a judge placing the awards.

We will take our first class, Senior White Males: We will take for granted we have an even dozen in this class. Before this class is brought on the table we should be provided with a judging box, each compartment large enough that the pig can be seen from all sides (the box to my liking should be six compartments long, two compartments deep, with each compartment at least six inches wide by twelve long and not over five inches high). We now place the twelve pigs in the twelve compartments. Our first duty is to eliminate those pigs that do not conform to our standard. We find two with straight ears, two more with long, sharp noses, one with a rough, dirty coat, unpresentable for the showroom, leaving us seven good, well-formed pigs.

Looking these over carefully, we find several slight faults, one with ears too erect, another with a small, sleepy eye, another with narrow shoulders, another with a nose too straight and long.

Here we call for a box about 10 inches wide by 12 to 18 inches long and will set up at least 8 to 16 inches over our judging table. This box is used to place our pigs upon—one, two, three or four at a time. They will sit quietly and not be running all over like, as if left on the table for comparison; besides, they are all lifted closer to our eye and up more prominent, so we can see their style, carriage, form and color, and get a better light.

JUDGE LEWIS S. J. GRIFFIN

Our next move now is to compare these three or four pigs, showing their weaknesses mentioned before, to see if any further weakness can be found; if not, to consider which is the most or farthest from perfection, according to our standard. After we have eliminated down to five, it is then our duty to compare these pigs, point for point, one against the other, for further weakness, ever keeping in mind the perfect pig, which should be strong in the following points:

Type: What is type? An animal that has graceful form, prominent outlines, showing a well-developed back,

PROFIT IN GUINEA PIGS

broad shoulders, high crown, thick neck, well-carried ears, a good short, blunt Roman nose, and one that stands up well in front with head up; eyes bold, large and as prominent as possible. There is nothing that pleases a judge more than to find a pig that is strong in type and will stand up to the touch of the judge's finger under the pig's jaws and show off his type and stand as if he knew what was expected and was proud of his ancestors' blood that he possessed. At this point we have decided which pig of the five has the best type and style, also eyes, ears and nose.

As this is the white class, color usually is almost equal except ears, and in many cases we are able to decide the winner by his ear color, taking other points equal that have before been decided upon. The ear must be clean, bright flesh color, free from stain, smut, etc.

Size of the pig is very important. The larger and more developed the pig in the Senior Class usually the better type he is able to present, and in most cases will show a better crown and broader shoulders at two years or older than a younger pig, but usually with age they develop coarser hair and usually not as smooth and soft a coat.

Having now placed our first, second, third, fourth and fifth in this Senior Class of Whites, we are ready to proceed to other classes. After finishing the whites, the color question takes a more prominent part.

In blacks, we must have blacks, the more dense, with a bright luster, the better, with the black carried clear down to the skin, not a brown, bluish undercast. Further, some blacks have not a good body color, but a brown, dusty stomach color. This should be cut severely, for when judging black make them black, with type and points as given in the white class combined. Personally, I would rather favor a black with one or two stray off-colored hairs than one with a brownish cast or poor type.

In the red classes, make the reds be red, not brown or rusty red. The red should have the fire and brightness

PROFIT IN GUINEA PIGS

to it, similar to a rich bright ripe tomato, not a dull dead brownish or yellow red.

In chocolates they should be chocolate, with good clear clean ears, a uniform chocolate color all over, not in patches.

The Golden Agouti should be reasonably dark to carry the rich color. It should be cut clean on each side of stomach and carry well under the front and back legs, and do not allow the red stomach color to show or streak up before and back of the legs. The circle about the eyes

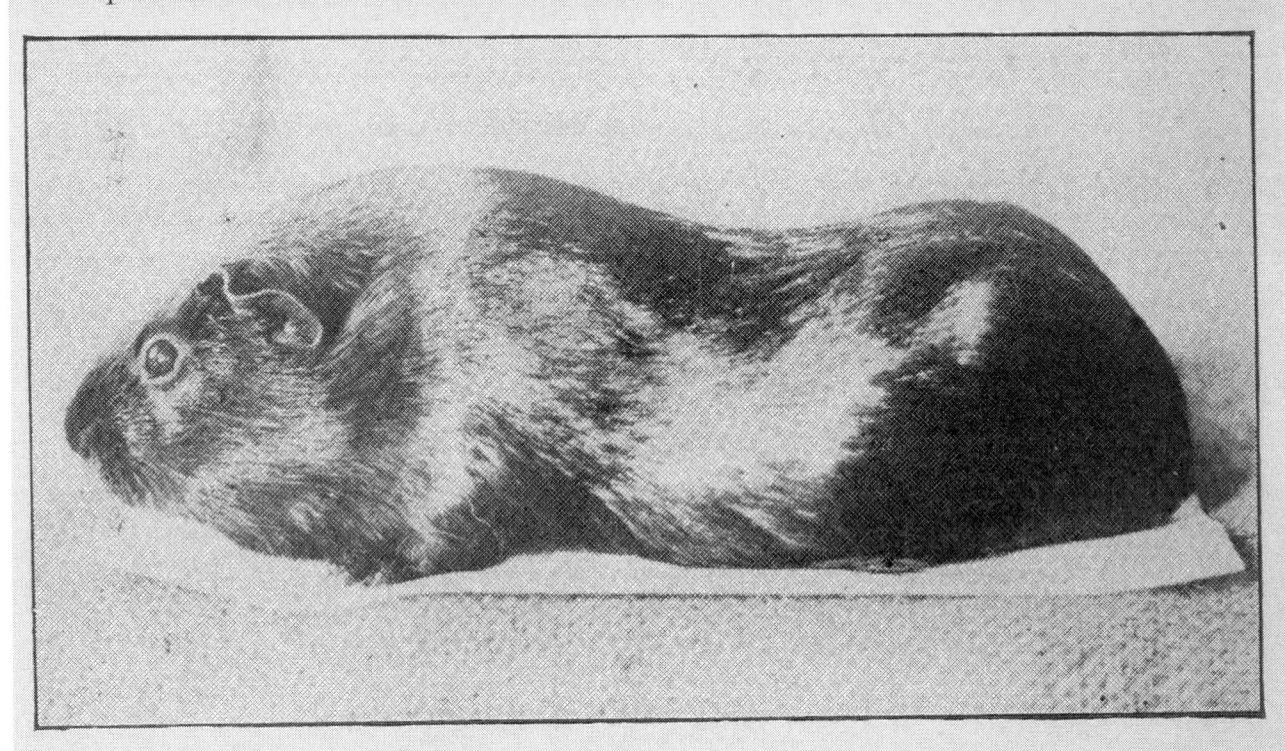

BLACK IMPORTED BOAR

as small as possible, and the color of the stomach to be a rich red clear to the skin, not dark smudgy under color.

The Silver Agouti, likewise, should be uniform, with stomach color cut clean as in the Goldens. The entire body color should be a bright steel and not show the reddish cast as seen in so many Silvers. The owners of Silvers should handle them often, for usually they are very wild and do not show off their best points.

PROFIT IN GUINEA PIGS

The cream pig should conform as to type and style almost like the white, except eye, which should be dark. The color of a good cream is all important. This should be a light shade of cream, rather than the dark yellowish or reddish brown we so often see. Keep your color as light as possible, with the color carried down deep to the skin, with all type possible.

Before closing this article a few suggestions to the new exhibitor may help him in the showroom.

First, remember a big, bold, prominent eye is all important and the bolder and larger it stands out the better. Next, all type possible, with the color you are breeding to be bright and fiery and dense and the same color throughout. Take a lead pencil and rub the hair back against the coat so as to see to the skin and see that you have a bright, clean color, not dark and smudgy.

Next, get all the size you can. When a pig is robust and heavy it usually is in good condition.

Now for a good start for the showroom. When your pigs are born, place the mother with one or two other cheap sows and remove their young in order to give the nourishment from the two or three mothers to the young, and see the difference in these young at four months against those left with their own mother. Further, give them all they can eat of both green and dry feed at all times. Milk and bran also is a big help.

Next, for condition of fur, use fine prairie hay, but before filling your pens where show stock is kept, wash this hay thoroughly and dry properly, bury your stock in this hay so they can run through this clean hay and use it as a brush to brighten and clean the fur.

Last but not least, handle your stock every chance you can, train them to sit quietly on a box and pose in whatever position they are placed. Above all, teach your

PROFIT IN GUINEA PIGS

animal to sit upright with the head erect and look you square in the face. This shows off the crown, back arch and head to best advantage.

A last warning in exhibiting solid colored pigs, use your pencil and rub the hair or fur the wrong way under the jaws, on the breast between front legs and inside of hind legs for patches of off-colored hairs. These are usually the places overlooked by the novice and oftimes by an old exhibitor. These off-colored patches will disqualify your pig.

MICKEY INSPECTING THE PIGS

PROFIT IN GUINEA PIGS

The Guinea Pig Industry

By C. S. Gibson, Chief Judge, N. B. & F. A., Inc.
Elwood, Indiana

When we mention Cavies only a few people really know what we are trying to describe, but if we say "Guinea Pigs" nearly every one knows, for only a few people have not heard of the popular little Guinea Pigs.

The Cavy industry has always been a large and profitable one in the East, Middle West, and now California ranks as the leading state over all other states in the number of Cavies raised within its boundaries. This wonderful increase in the number of cavy breeders in California was brought about through the earnest endeavors of America's foremost cavy breeder, Dr. Roberts of Hollywood. Dr. Roberts, single-handed, started thousands of people raising this profitable little animal and today the Cavy takes its place with the poultry, rabbits, fruit and other things which enter largely into making a living for many people in California.

For a number of years the Cavy was looked upon as a pastime or sort of a joke with big business people, but since the laboratory has been using them in large numbers the American public realizes what an important industry it has become.

If it had not been for the Cavies some of our most wonderful serums would never have been discovered.

During the late war they were also used extensively for detecting gas before it would reach the lines. They would be placed out ahead of the front trenches and always gave warning to the troops.

PROFIT IN GUINEA PIGS

A great many people also claim to have been cured of rheumatism by simply making a bedfellow of the Cavy.

They are also used for exhibitions and a number of cases are on record where they have brought enormous prices.

CHAS. S. GIBSON
Chief Judge and Organizer of the National
Breeders and Fanciers' Association, Inc.

For laboratory experimental purposes the short-haired English are the ones used and come in the following colors: Broken Colors, Red, Black, White, Cream,

PROFIT IN GUINEA PIGS

Chocolate, Tortoise and White, Golden Agouti and Silver Agouti. These varieties are also used as exhibition types.

The Abyssinian are the rough, wiry Cavies with rosettes. They also come in solid and broken colors.

To a large number of people the beautiful Peruvian long-hair is the finest of all exhibition cavies.

The cost of producing Cavies is so small and the profit so large we find the industry growing in leaps and bounds.

We find the women are taking to this new industry and it affords them much pleasure as well as profit.

Very few of the Cavy breeders at the present time can begin to supply the demand, so the future of this industry looks very bright indeed.

Cavies Are Always Contented, Easily Raised, Cared for and Shipped.

PROFIT IN GUINEA PIGS

Climate and Cavies

By ED. G. HABERSTROH, Cavy Expert,
2140 South 35th Ave., Omaha, Neb.

In territories where they experience extremely cold weather, as in the northern states, Cavies require different housing, and you should build warm quarters for them. However, cavies are not affected a great deal by heat or cold, but it is well that you protect them in the winter months by placing them in the basement near your furnace; if you are a city raiser, you will find this a very convenient place for them, and is handy in caring for them at the same time that you care for the furnace.

Cavies have no odor whatsoever if their hutches are kept dry and are cleaned at least once a week. If you are located on a farm and have cattle or horses, it is well that you build your hutches in the same barn you keep the livestock, for the animal heat from the stock will keep them warm.

Should you be a cavy raiser on a fairly large scale and have a hundred breeding sows or more, you should have a stove in your caviary that will take away the chill. However, many breeders keep their stock out of doors winter and summer with no bad results, while others experience a considerable loss. Personally, I believe that cavies should be cared for and protected from the cold the same as any other animal, and they will repay you a thousand-fold by caring for them in the proper manner.

Always have plenty of clean bedding in the hutches during cold spells if you are not located so that you can have warm quarters for them.

PROFIT IN GUINEA PIGS

Many raisers do not water cavies in the winter time, providing they can secure green foodstuff, such as carrots, beets, squash or any other vegetables which contain water, as most of these vegetables contain about 95 per cent water, and this is sufficient to care for their needs.

ED G. HABERSTROH
Cavy Expert
2140 South 35th Ave., Omaha, Neb.

If you expect to have over one hundred breeding sows, it would be well that you erect a building about 10 feet wide by 20 feet long with a slanting roof, using tar paper for sheeting the inside of the building. A building of the above dimensions will house 500 breeding sows and can be put up at a cost of about $150. This may vary, according to the grade of material that you use. It is best to

PROFIT IN GUINEA PIGS

have a wood floor in the building, or a dirt floor will do if you do not want to go to the expense of putting in a wooden floor. However, many breeders have cement floors, but in the winter this is cold and sometimes damp. Build your hutches 2 feet by 4 feet, using two trays in a hutch, which are two feet square. This will make the

Cavies Are the Greatest Mothers in the World. Note the Pose of the Mother Cavy So as Not to Lie on the Young.

cleaning of the hutches very easy and you will not need to handle your cavies, for in handling them it scares them and they sometimes have premature young caused by fright.

Cavies can be raised in any climate in the United States, only using judgment as to the territory where you are located. They are the easiest of all animals to raise and the most profitable, providing you have an established market for your stock, and the demand for good stock is advancing by leaps and bounds.

PROFIT IN GUINEA PIGS

The Cavy Industry of the South

OTTO MARTIN LOCKE, Jr.,
Southern Cavy Expert, New Braunfels, Texas

When we speak of the South we generally have Texas in mind simply because it is the biggest state in the Union. The South may not be as highly developed in the cavy industry as the other parts of America, but it is coming along good and in a few years I hope to see it on the map.

So many people ask me how I keep my cavies, as they state that they never saw any plans of Southern cavy hutches. I build a nice rain and draft proof shed, better a nice little house wherein you can make the pens successfully, as it is not best to keep cavies out of doors here in winter.

In summer it is different. Then they may be turned loose on courts and they will be as contented as can be.

The feed problem is not hard in the South, as we can plant carrots the year round and they will do well. And carrots is a food cavies like. Alfalfa can also be grown the year round, but I have tried some of the new Hubam clover, have bought some pedigreed seed from the originators and find it is wonderful for cavies and grows like weeds.

We also feed milkweeds and thistles to cavies and they are the finest foods, in fact cavies fed with these two weeds grew exceptionally fast.

Real often I receive inquiries as follows: "Is there a profit in raising cavies in the South?" To these I reply,

PROFIT IN GUINEA PIGS

"Yes, there is a good profit in the raising of cavies in the South, and also a great pleasure!"

Have bred cavies of all breeds and colors successfully ever since 1912 and find the South is just the ideal spot for cavies. They thrive so wonderfully in our sunny South and I highly recommend the Southern people to take more interest in this noble animal. Yes, an animal

OTTO MARTIN LOCKE, Jr.,

that gives its blood and life to let human beings live! The cavy makes a wonderful pet and cavy meat is very good.

The cavy industry in the South is not at all developed as much as in other parts of America simply because pub-

PROFIT IN GUINEA PIGS

licity is lacking. I hope that through this book many people will be interested in cavies and join us in this great industry.

Cavies can be raised successfully in outdoor hutches in the South, provided they are damp and draft proof. Cavies can stand a good deal of cold, but they cannot stand drafts or damp hutches. The best way to raise cavies in the South is to build a house about 12x14 and have the hutches in this house in tiers. Of course, sufficient light and ventilation is essential and anyone can make a nice caviary.

About the feeding problems of cavies, we do not have to worry, as we can raise green feed the year round here.

Another good feed for cavies is alfalfa, which may either be fed green or cured. Green cornstalks are also excellent feeds for cavies and they will eat them whole. Cavies also do well on green or dried oats.

I never feed my cavies mashes, as a mash will spoil within an hour if the cavies do not eat them. Whole and rolled oats are good cavy feeds, as well as rolled barley. Wheat bran is an excellent food for cavies.

So in conclusion I say there is a great deal of profit in raising cavies in the South. More power to the cavy.

JOIN THE
Western Cavy Breeders' Association

The Association Worth While
Colorado Springs, Colorado

What is it? Who is it?

LIVE CAVY BREEDERS AND FANCIERS.

Why is it?

It is its set purpose to promote the breeding of cavies in a profitable way—to boost the cavy in the showrooms by giving cash prizes to members at official shows—to boost and promote the cavy commercially as food in competition with poultry and rabbits. To have the now existing express rates reduced to a level with rabbits and poultry. We have said a great deal here in a few words. To accomplish this end we need your co-operation as a breeder, fancier and brother in the game.

WHEN? Right now if you are alive and a booster.

We want you. You want us. We also need your dollar. We need it along with all the rest we can get to accomplish the many good things we have in view for the benefit of the cavy industry and the man or woman therein engaged. Are you not willing to put a dollar a year against the time and labor our officers and members are devoting for the good of the cavy industry?

Let us send you a membership card in "The Association Worth While."

A one dollar bill or your personal check will do the trick. Send same to E. D. Wheeler, Secretary, Western Cavy Breeders' Association, Colorado Springs, Colorado.

Please mention this book when sending for application.

Showing Convenient Shipping Pens, or Can Be Used to Place Young in When Weaning Them

C -- is for CAVIES--that make money for you;

A -- is for ASSOCIATION--that will help you, too,

V -- is for VARIETY--which ever you choose;

I -- is for INVESTMENT--which you will not loose,

E -- is for EVERYONE--you can be in the game;

S -- is for SATISFACTION--for you will receive same.

By DR. J. A. ROBERTS.

Cavy Supplies - Order Them Today

Health Salt Spools a Necessity for Cavies. You Will Surely Need Them.

Per dozen $1.20

JARS—YOU NEED THESE

Jars, each.....................................$ .25
1 dozen or more, each........................ .20

ROBERTS HUTCH CARDS

For marking and tabulating cavies. Each card full data for a year.

Per dozen...................................$ .12

ROBERTS CAVY EAR TAGS

Made of aluminum. Numbers stamped in the metal. Attach by punching a hole in the ear of the cavy, insert tag and then the washer, bend prongs to hold in place.

Per dozen...................................$ .25
Ear Tag Punches, each..................... .50

Dr. J. A. Roberts' Disinfectene is a combination of harmless ingredients compounded after years of experiment and is especially adapted for use with all kinds of pet stock. It is the best product of its kind on the market. It can be used without injury on any kind of livestock or poultry.

Price, per one-quart can.....................$1.00
Sprayers, one pint capacity................... .75

ROBERTS HEALTHENE

To be used in drinking water for cavies if they have a cold or are sickly. Just a teaspoonful in a quart of water is a preventive against colds, pneumonia, bowel trouble, etc. Full directions on each can.

Price, per one-pint can......................$1.00

HUTCH CLEANERS

Made of steel and is a wonderful help in making hutch cleaning easy.

Price, each..................................$1.00

CAVY LICE POWDER

Used with powder gun and prepared especially for cavies. Directions on package.

Price, 1-lb. carton..........................$ .50
Jumbo Powder Gun............................ .50

CAVY SULPHUR TONIC

For purifying the blood, keeping the digestive system healthy. Recommended to counteract the effect of diseases, as abscesses, boils, skin eruptions.

Price, 1-lb. carton..........................$ .50

CAVY CONDITIONER

Composed of mixed grains and herbs essential to building up and strengthening the system and general health of the cavy.

Price, 10-lb. sacks..........................$ .50

DR. J. A. ROBERTS LABORATORIES, Inc.
6634 Sunset Boulevard   HOLLYWOOD, CAL.

2140 South 35th Avenue
Omaha, Nebraska

Raise Guinea Pigs for Us

WE SUPPLY STOCK AND GIVE YOU A CONTRACT

Send 25 cents for big booklet giving you information and telling you about Cavies.

ED HABERSTROH, Manager

Established 15 Years

Please mention this book when writing.

BIG BOOK ON RABBITS

The Greatest Book
ever written on this subject

by

CHIEF JUDGE CHAS. S. GIBSON

Organizer of

THE

National Breeders and Fanciers Association

INCORPORATED

If You Are Interested in the Rabbit Industry You Should Have This Great Book

Send One Dollar For Your Copy to

Chas. S. Gibson Dept. R, Elwood, Indiana

Please mention this book when writing.

WE BUY

Thousands of CAVIES (Guinea Pigs) every year raised from foundation stock supplied by us. Why not get into this **clean, profitable, pleasant** business and make **big money.**

Pays for Herself Three Times a Year

Cavies are not hard to raise and take but little space; the work connected with it is clean and pleasant and each sow pays for herself three times a year for between eight and nine years. She costs $2.50 and should net you between $7.50 and $8.00. They are doing it for hundreds of our raisers.

What Counts Most When You Make a Purchase

It is the integrity and character of the persons with whom you deal. We have been established for over fifteen years. In all that time our service has been consistent and our dealings fair.

OUR CONTRACT

Means much to our raisers. It gives them a guaranteed market. Call on us or send 25 cents for booklet—

How to Make $2,000 a Year

Dr. J. A. Roberts, Pres.   H. G. Gaussen, Sec'y & Treas.

Dr. J. A. Roberts Laboratories
Incorporated

6634 Sunset Boulevard

Hollywood, Calif.

SUBSCRIBE NOW

For the Leading Pet Stock Journal

By All Means You Should Have
This Valuable Journal

Published Monthly $1.00 per Year

Outdoor Enterprises
for Pleasure and Profit

Dept. R., 115 E. 31st St., Kansas City, Mo.

Please mention this book when sending subscription

BREEDERS ALL OVER

Are Making Big Profits
Selling This Book

Profits in Guinea Pigs

To Your Friends and Customers in Connection With Your Business

---

WRITE FOR SPECIAL
DEALERS' PRICE

DR. J. A. ROBERTS
6634 Sunset Boulevard
Hollywood, California

Profit in CAVIES or **GUINEA PIGS**
by Dr. J. A. Roberts

The Greatest
Book on Cavies
Ever Published

Price $1.50

Printed in Great Britain
by Amazon